SmartMatch
Alliances

D0735185

Alliances.SmartMatch

Achieve Extraordinary Business Growth and Success!

JUDY FELD and ERNEST F. ORIENTE

JumpingJack Publishing

Park City, UT

Copyright © 2002 by Judy Feld and Ernest F. Oriente.

All rights reserved. No part of this book may be reproduced or transmitted in any form or by any means, electronic or mechanical, including photocopying, recording, or by any information storage and retrieval system, without permission in writing from the publisher.

Published by
JumpingJack Publishing
Park City, Utah

Publisher's Cataloging-in-Publication Data
Feld, Judy.
    SmartMatch alliances : achieve extraordinary business
    growth and success / Judy Feld, Ernest F. Oriente.
    — Park City, Utah : JumpingJack Publishing, 2002.

        p. ; cm.
    ISBN 0-9722283-0-6

    1. Strategic alliances (Business) 2. Partnership. 3. Business
    networks. 4. Management. I. Oriente, Ernest F. I. Title.

HD69.S8 F45   2002   2002109222
658   —dc21   0209

Printed in the United States of America

06 05 04 03 02 • 5 4 3 2 1

Front cover and interior graphics by:
The Business Lab, *www.thebusinesslab.com*

Contents

Acknowledgments

We would like to acknowledge the substantial help we had in creating this book. Over the years, we have been greatly inspired by our clients around the world, TeleForum participants, and the feedback from our E-newsletter subscribers. We thank all of you. In a significant way, each of you has touched our lives.

A special thanks to our brilliant editor Diana Morris who was able to pull together thousands of alliance concepts and ideas and deliver a cohesive, step-by-step journey into the world of SmartMatch Alliances. She is certainly a gift in our lives . . . and we will forever be touched by her love, support, and wisdom.

Professionally, we would like to thank our coaching colleagues who have shared their ideas selflessly, inspired us with their dedication, motivated us to work smarter and play harder . . . and encouraged us to write this book. We are honored to be part of the community of coaches and hope that our humble contribution reflects well on a profession that has such a positive impact on the lives of so many people and businesses.

To our thousands of clients around the world, thank you for being willing to build SmartMatch Alliances . . . and for being as excited as we are about the success they have generated.

To our wonderful families, thank you for the support and understanding, both tacit and visible, as we wrote this book. You knew this was a labor of love, and you let us pursue our passion. More than paper and glue, it is your love and patience that hold this book together. We love each of you . . . and thank you for being in our lives.

Preface

*I*n my various leadership roles at the NFL and Showtime, I've seen firsthand how strategic alliances produce powerful results for alliance partners . . . the ultimate win-win.

This trend has continued to gather a great deal of momentum in recent years, with good reason: *strategic alliances work.* Businesses of all sizes benefit significantly from the powerful synergies well-designed alliances deliver—and this book definitively brings to readers the enhanced power of SmartMatch Alliances.

Ernest Oriente and Judy Feld provide a detailed, step-by-step process—going beyond traditional alliance principles—for creating exponential success in your business and career. Their own successful alliance, established in 1996, is a real-life, real-time example of the power of this concept to transform your career, your business . . . and your life.

As great business coaches, Ernest and Judy provide a solid game plan, and paint a compelling picture of the goal: a flourishing business, a prosperous career. In sports, when you combine an excellent game plan with great motivation, the result most often is a well-deserved victory . . . a sensational win. SmartMatch Alliances have the potential to create this type of win for you.

Enjoy the book, and best of luck to you with your SmartMatch Alliances.

By Neil Austrian,
Former NFL President and Chief Operating Officer
Former Showtime/The Movie Channel Chairman and Chief Executive Officer

Welcome!

*"If you advance confidently in the direction of your dreams,
and endeavor to live the life that you've imagined,
you will meet with a success unexpected in common hours."*

— Henry David Thoreau, author, philosopher, naturalist

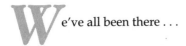e've all been there . . .

- "How am I supposed to go out and get new business when all I have time to do is work on the business I already have?"
- "Marketing is so expensive . . . and poor results don't help! I mailed 10,000 brochures and received no responses."
- "I'm struggling to find solid strategies for adding new subscribers to my E-newsletter while respecting standards of 'Netiquette' and privacy."
- "My sales cycle seems to take forever. I may spend three full days writing and delivering a proposal. Then I call the prospect ten times to follow up and get no response. It's maddening!"

The list continues. Anyone running a small or mid-sized business or justifying a corporate budget knows all too well the pain of low-impact, high-priced sales and marketing efforts.

What on earth is happening?

In a word—CLUTTER. Massive amounts of information overwhelm us . . . by one researcher's count, each day more than 7,000 advertising impressions reach an individual living in a typical suburban town. Contact information on a single consumer can be—and often is—shared with hundreds, maybe thousands of direct marketing organizations that will start spewing out more mail to that consumer in short order, like it or not.

Choices abound. Want to buy a car? Invest in a mutual fund? Make spaghetti tonight? Watch a TV program? Get a better mortgage?

In each case, you have anywhere from 50 to 5,000 choices . . . and not all of them are good.

The fact that we live in a time-starved world only compounds the clutter problem. Today, most people won't spend precious time and money experimenting with new brands or trying unfamiliar products, services, providers, or ideas. It's easier and takes less time to use familiar brands and buy from the organizations they know and trust.

What's a success-minded purveyor of superior products, top-notch services, and solid ideas to do?

What if we told you there's a way you can break through the clutter and connect directly with big-ticket buyers and high-potential prospects . . . a means of attracting more clients, customers, and prospects than you've ever imagined? A way to partner and learn from like-minded people and companies in your profession, industry, niches, and specialties? A method of establishing a strong, memorable brand for yourself, your company, your products, and your services? A business-building strategy that's low- to no-risk and always win-win . . . one in which the only limits are your own imagination, creativity, and energy?

There is.

In the simple act of opening this book, you've opened the door to a new world, a world in which you—

get better prospects . . .

to come to you . . .

in greater numbers . . .

faster than ever before.

A world in which you charge more . . . earn more . . . and have more fun!

It's the world of SmartMatch Alliances™.

 OUR STORY

Not too long ago, perhaps just like you, we sat in our respective offices building our respective worldwide coaching businesses. We created these businesses in the quest for independence, autonomy, and creativity. And, perhaps like you, we had drawn on our corporate experiences, entrepreneurial spirit, and enthusiasm, and we had succeeded . . . to a point.

But our journey had just begun. On each of our minds—perhaps just like yours—was a simple question:

"What's next?"

It was a question that opened our minds . . . and opened the door. In the Winter of 1996, we happened to "meet" on a virtual teleconference business seminar. In the months that followed, we shared our respective dreams, communicating by E-mail and phone. Judy wanted to touch thousands of business owners and corporate leaders from her "intergalactic" headquarters. Ernest dreamed of building a global coaching business while living at the base of a ski resort and traveling around the world.

We began Coaching Success™ (www.coachingsuccess. com), our own strategic alliance, and instantly invited new freedoms, ideas, and possibilities into our lives and our businesses. Together, we created TeleForums™, our highly profitable, signature approach to using teleconference technology to upskill eager entrepreneurs, business owners, and enterprising corporate employees on how to be more successful in every aspect of their careers and professions and how to create strategic alliances that expand their businesses and increase their success.

Our work and our lives changed—permanently. It was as if we walked through a gate that opened in only one direction and then closed and locked behind us. Once we stepped through and entered the world of strategic alliances, new vistas opened before us. We saw a rainbow of opportunities, and we quickly realized the power we had to build a much brighter future as a team.

Coaching Success has been the success model and test laboratory for the hundreds of strategic alliances we've established with and for client organizations and companies around the world. We coined the term SmartMatch Alliances™ to describe this powerful business model.

Today, we're each more successful than we ever dreamed. We have clients, friends, and colleagues around the world. Our monthly E-newsletter has more than 12,000 subscribers in 70-plus countries. We've appeared in a wide variety of periodicals, including *The New York Times, Fast Company, The LA Times, Fortune, BusinessWeek, Self Employed America, Financial Times,* and *Working Woman.* We're also published in hundreds of trade and industry magazines and websites each month.

As a result of this marketing visibility, in addition to creating great businesses, we've been able to create great lives for ourselves and our families. We love and honor ease, simplicity, and effortless marketing. 99 percent of our work (There are rare exceptions!) is done from the convenience and comfort of our own specially-designed offices. We've never made a cold call or directly solicited business for our coaching services. And we have eliminated commuting from our lives . . . need we say more?

Come, see the world through our eyes, and grow with us in excitement, passion, and joy for your work and your life.

You CAN build the success you've dreamed of and live the life you've imagined . . . and never look back!

 ## INSIDE SMARTMATCH ALLIANCES

In the pages of this book, we provide a no-nonsense process for maximizing this success-building tool, show you how to create SmartMatch Alliances and integrate them into your business strategy, and introduce you to some of the people who are meeting with tremendous success doing just that.

This book is organized around our signature eight-step approach to building SmartMatch Alliances, a method developed in the process of creating hundreds of these powerful alliances for ourselves and for our coaching clients around the world.

We've included SmartMatch Alliance worksheets, checklists, brainstorming tools, sample language for conversations and correspondence with your potential SmartMatch Alliance partners, our SmartNotes success tips, frequently asked questions, and much more.

To get the absolute most out of every chapter of *Smart-Match Alliances*, we suggest keeping a notebook to serve as your *Alliance Journal*, a place to record your notes and ideas about building SmartMatch Alliances. You might also visit our website www.coachingsuccess.com to purchase and immediately download an *Alliance Journal* which we created as a companion workbook to the SmartMatch Alliance building process.

Keeping an *Alliance Journal* will enable you to preserve the clean pages in this book for ongoing use as you build each new SmartMatch Alliance. Keep your *Alliance Journal* accessible as you work through each of the steps in the Smart-Match Alliance building process.

You might also want to create a SmartMatch Alliances folder in which to keep your *Alliance Journal* as well as any

An Important Note on Client Stories

The people and stories in this book are real. We have changed names and other identifying information in order to protect our clients' privacy.

other notes, articles, and the like that support the creation of powerful, targeted SmartMatch Alliances.

Please enjoy every page of our book. Our dream is to expand your horizons, help you flex new muscles, and . . . most important of all . . . help you find greater joy and fulfillment in your work and life.

SmartMatch Alliances is for and about you, your business, your career, your growth and success. We wish you the very best. Good luck!

Your Coaches,
Ernest and Judy
September 2002

Giant Steps,
an Introduction

*"There is one thing stronger than all the armies in the world,
and that is an idea whose time has come."*

—VICTOR HUGO, 19TH CENTURY NOVELIST

On a sun-drenched afternoon late in the spring of 1450, Johannes Guttenberg was enjoying himself at a local wine festival outside his hometown
of Mainz, Germany. He noted the mechanics of the wine press and (perhaps after
imbibing a glass or two) believed he could combine the press with the techniques
of using dies for coin punching to produce a printed page.

With that slight inspiration, Guttenberg created the first movable printing
press, and the rest, as they say, is history.

Many would declare the printing press the most important development of
the last millennium. It ushered in the era of mass communication, and the world
was never the same. Religion, science, politics, and business were all transformed
by the power of the press and its ability to quickly create works that could be
spread throughout the land. Just 50 years after its development, more than 1,000
presses could be found in more than 200 locations throughout Europe.

The printing press made it easier and faster to disseminate information, and, more importantly: it connected people, creating communities of political thinkers, scientists, and philosophers.

People connecting with each other and sharing information for mutual benefit . . .

Hold that thought.

Fast forward 550-plus years, and zoom in on you, reading this book.

Welcome to the second communication revolution—the one taking place right now!—a time in which information circumnavigates the globe with a mouse click. The idea of community has changed from your neighbors next door to your neighbors in the next hemisphere. Ours is an age of unlimited information, instant access, and communities of thinkers and doers as large as our minds (and our bandwidths!) will permit.

On the surface, this revolution—quite clearly the defining event of this millennium thus far—is about making information available to the masses faster than ever before. As a result of the Internet becoming more easily (and more frequently) used by the general public in the mid-1990s, millions of websites have been created by people and businesses in every corner of the world.

Yet it's below the surface where the real revolution is occurring. Just as with the printing press, the vehicle that enables information to be disseminated faster than ever—the Web—also enables us to create new communities and more intimate business relationships with a wider variety of people than ever before.

Once again, just like in Guttenberg's time, we see a quantum leap in the ways people connect with each other and share information for mutual benefit, a single development that has changed the world: "One small step," as astronaut Neil Armstrong said stepping onto the lunar surface, that becomes "one giant leap for mankind."

"Oh please!" We hear you scream. "I'm just trying to run a business here!"

And run it you will, while working less, earning more, meeting (and even surpassing) your budgetary goals, and having more fun in the process. We're about to show you how you can easily and profitably take advantage of today's technology, partner with success-minded people no matter where in the world they are, and spur your own imagination by building strategic alliances that let you—

get better prospects . . .
to come to you . . .
in greater numbers . . .
faster than ever before.

so you can charge more . . . earn more . . . and have more fun!

Alliances are powerful collaborations with success-minded individuals and businesses that catapult you and your company into a new era of growth in your life, career, and business. Alliance partners exchange some of the visibility vehicles they've created for themselves and their businesses in new, synergistic relationships with people and businesses around the corner or around the world—each a strategic alliance in which the whole is greater than the sum of its parts.

Within strategic alliances, you build relationships that enable you and your alliance partners to reach new, high-potential prospects, clients, and customers, often with a more complete and valuable product or service offering.

Your only must-haves are an entrepreneurial spirit, the ability to identify your own brand of "genius work" (you'll find much more on genius work starting on page 21), the willingness to think outside the box, and a deep understanding of what we call your PINS—your profession, industry, niches and specialties. (PINS are central to SmartMatch Alliance building. You'll find much more on this pivotal concept starting on page 31!).

Ultimately, this is a book about success—YOUR success—a book that will help you chart a course to your own dreams, on your own terms.

ALLIANCES . . . WITH A TWIST!

"None of us is as smart as all of us," said management guru Ken Blanchard in a beautiful, simple articulation of two alliance-building fundamentals: collaboration and brainstorming.

Strategic alliances have been around as long as people and businesses have worked together for mutual benefit. They've appeared as guilds, licensing agreements, cooperative merchandising arrangements (think of action figures from the latest Disney movie appearing in a McDonald's Happy Meal®), and every other form of business-to-business collaboration.

Today's strategic alliances have a decidedly modern twist. Did you know that companies whose brand names are household words for everything from ketchup to sneakers often don't manufacture their products? These giants have enormous networks of strategic alliances with other companies that manufacture and often package and distribute their products. They actually are virtual enterprises whose primary equity is the goodwill and reputation of their brand names and the marketing methods that support their ongoing brand-building efforts. They leverage technology to pull vendors and suppliers in from all over the world as needed and just-in-time, and then disband them quickly when circumstances and needs change.

Why? One reason and one reason only: this is the most efficient, profitable way to operate in a world of dizzying change, in which opportunities can, and often do, appear and disappear in the blink of an eye.

SmartMatch Alliances, our own approach to building strategic alliances, includes elements of this approach tailored to the hopes, dreams, and goals of our clients, who are small to mid-sized businesses and dynamic corporate leaders. We help these individuals and their companies build strategic alliances—quickly and intelligently . . . generating high-profit opportunities.

With proven strategies for bringing alliance partners together, we help businesses zero-in on better prospects in greater numbers. They begin to produce higher revenues and growth, as well as massive time and cost efficiencies (Imagine: no meetings! No flying across the country to deliver a presentation! No 20-page RFPs to complete! No 10-page legal documents to pore over . . . or pour coffee over!). Our clients who make use of the SmartMatch Alliance principles are no longer constrained by physical office space (We like to say they've conquered their "edifice complex"!), bricks and mortar factories, geography, time zones, the local labor pool, or national currencies.

They're ready, willing, and able to build profitable alliances, and they know where to look . . . regionally, nationally, and globally, inside specific professions, industries, niches, areas of specialty, and more. They're even capable of spotting opportunities for creating alliances with their own clients or customers.

In the pages that follow you'll meet some of them, people like:

- **John, the owner of a web-based training business that services companies with employees working internationally.** John dramatically increased sales and the size of his client base by forming a revenue-sharing alliance with a company that has sales relationships with Fortune 500 companies, thus generating $250,000 in new revenue.

- **Sarah, owner of a magazine that helps people age 50-plus find housing choices.** Sarah gained exposure and increased distribution by placing an issue of her magazine in a major drug store chain. Imprinted on the issue were the words, "Compliments of [the drug store]." Because of the increased exposure, Sarah sold $100,000 in new advertising. At the same time, the drug store chain gained goodwill and enhanced customer loyalty in the communities it serves.

- **Mitch, the president of a graphic design firm.** Mitch increased his client base by creating a SmartMatch Alliance with a printer. Mitch designed the printing firm's quarterly marketing pieces gratis—in a way that enables the firm to showcase its high-quality printing capabilities. In exchange, the firm placed his name and contact information on the marketing pieces and mailed them to its clients and prospects. Both gained exposure and new clients and significantly increased their revenues. At last count, Mitch reported $150,000 in new revenue—and still growing!—as a direct result of this alliance.

While each story is unique, common themes come into sharp relief. SmartMatch Alliances are:

- **Win-win.** Each alliance partner benefits and thrives.
- **Low- to no-risk.** Usually, alliance partners don't spend money unless they're making money, or as we like to say . . . revenues first . . . expenses second!
- **Easy to develop.** The simpler, the better.
- **High leverage.** A small investment of time and effort yields big results.
- **Low- or no-cost.** Partners substitute creative thinking for big money.
- **Flexible.** Solid alliances are easy-in, easy-out, and easy-to-revise.
- **Just-in-time.** No inventory to build and store, no extra resources needed . . . no hassles!
- **Profitable.** Some solid business math: great leverage + high visibility = big profits.
- **Fun.** And why not?

We begin with a focused exploration of the key features and elemental qualities of this **Business Breakthrough . . .**

one

A Business Breakthrough

"Dream of success and happy victory!"

—WILLIAM SHAKESPEARE, POET AND PLAYWRIGHT
KING RICHARD III, ACT V, SCENE III

W hile the concept is somewhat new to today's business owners and managers who have cut their teeth on "beating the competition" or "going it alone," alliances have been around in one form or another for a long time. Webster's Dictionary defines an alliance as "an association to further the common interests of its members." You help me, I help you, we both get something we want. Win-win.

Our working definition of a SmartMatch Alliance is an "arrangement between two or more businesses to exchange something of equal value with the aim of increasing the visibility, sales, and profits of each alliance partner."

The operative words are "exchange" and "equal value." (Both concepts are essential to understanding the Exchange of Value or EOV . . . a fundamental principle behind SmartMatch Alliances. You'll find much more on EOVs starting on page 80.)

Let's begin with exchange. "Exchange" is key because each partner must bring something to the alliance aimed at increasing the exposure, visibility, and revenues of the other. Here's a classic example: Business A and Business B form a strategic alliance in which they agree that A will pay B if B presents and sells A's products to its clients. As a result both A and B gain customers and increase their revenues.

"Equal value" is important because what is exchanged should create a solid win for each alliance partner. If one side offers more than the other, the alliance will produce uneven results. There must be reciprocity in equal measure in order for the alliance to fulfill its promise of equal upside potential.

Business A and Business B might decide to display each other's marketing materials in their respective establishments . . . a simple example of a no-risk, equal value exchange, and a clear win-win. To increase the equal value exchange, A and B might also decide to link their websites, enclose the other's marketing material in their mailings, and/or share a booth at an industry trade show.

Next we have the term "low- to no-risk." It's important to acknowledge that not every alliance is a success. Sometimes partners renege. On occasion, the chemistry is off. But alliances defy the maxim "Nothing ventured, nothing gained" by enabling alliance partners to leverage a small upfront investment of time into substantial gains in sales and profitability. Perhaps the alliance maxim should read: "Something really simple ventured, something really big gained, and absolutely nothing lost." (Not quite as catchy as the original, but it makes the point!)

The definition of alliances isn't complete without the concept of "leverage." Leverage is, in simple terms, a small investment of time, money, or any other resource that produces a disproportionately large return. Done right, a Smart-Match Alliance will leverage the marketing visibility of each alliance partner to bring the other substantial increases in visibility, exposure—and therefore sales—of their products and services.

BREAK THROUGH YOUR EARNINGS CEILING

No less a business guru than Peter Drucker noted, not simply a surge in alliances, but a "worldwide restructuring" occurring in the form of strategic alliances.

The value of alliances has been placed in the trillions and is expected to grow to between $30 and $50 trillion within five years. One study found that more than 20 percent of the revenue generated by the top 2,000 U.S. and European companies annually comes from alliances. Moreover, these same companies earn higher return on investment (ROI) and return on equity (ROE)—two critical measures of business success—on their alliances than on their core businesses.

This is big stuff!

And just as they have for thousands of businesses, from corporate giants to entrepreneurial upstarts, strategic alliances can help you break through your earnings ceiling in an easy-to-manage, low- to no-risk fashion. In addition, strategic alliances are rapidly becoming the accepted business tool to grow your company without committing yourself to expensive formal expansions into new markets.

AN ALLIANCE *ISN'T* . . .

Strategic alliances are a powerful business expansion strategy with many of the benefits and few, if any, of the risks of traditional expansion strategies. SmartMatch Alliances can be contrasted with . . .

> *Networking.* Networking efforts increase your visibility, no strings attached. In its simplest form, networking is done by exchanging one business card for another. You might conduct this exchange by joining your local Chamber of Commerce or attending a monthly luncheon given by your professional or

industry association. Perhaps you travel across the country or around the world to attend a conference or trade show in order to meet and speak to a number of people at once. By comparison, a SmartMatch Alliance is designed around marketing and visibility vehicles that enable you to reach tens of thousands (or more) potential buyers in one initiative. You can't swap 10,000 business cards at a Chamber of Commerce meeting, but you can reach 10,000 new, high-potential prospects through a SmartMatch Alliance!

A merger or an acquisition. These are complex business deals in which each company's structure changes—permanently. SmartMatch Alliances, in contrast, do

Q: Are strategic alliances and leads groups the same thing?

A: While both concepts work to increase exposure, prospects and sales, strategic alliances provide far more leverage. Alliances enable you to reach tens of thousands of prospects, clients, and customers. By comparison, a leads group might provide 1 to 15 leads a month . . . if you're lucky.

Strategic alliances also differ in their:
- Reach. Alliances enable you to play globally. Leads groups, by definition, are constrained by local or regional reach.
- Quality. Alliances generate exposure to your perfect marketing niches, while leads groups provide more generic leads—whoever is "available."
- Creativity. Alliances generate more than exposure. They provide a vehicle for creative new ideas and a view toward the future. In contrast, leads are a simple, practical, in-the-present exchange of value.

not change the way you run your company. They're an add-on, a powerful complement to what you're already doing.

Outsourcing. Outsourcing is the purchase of non-core products and services from outside vendors and specialists. It is strictly a buyer-supplier relationship and a very clear quid pro quo: money in exchange for products and services. A SmartMatch Alliance, on the other hand, creates a business-building relationship between two or more companies in which money flows in every direction among alliance partners.

 PROOF POSITIVE

Mary, a Coaching Success client, is a business consultant who works exclusively with financial planners and brokers. Mary wanted to expand her list of clients. She contacted several owners of key industry websites and offered to host a Tele-Forum for their E-newsletter subscribers using our Smart-Match Alliance model (see pages 62 to 68 for a concise definition and strategies for hosting TeleForums). Her topic: business-building strategies for financial planners. In exchange, the website owners provided exposure for Mary and included invitations to her weekly TeleForums in their weekly newsletters.

After three years, this alliance is still running smoothly. Both sides continue to benefit. For her part, Mary has increased her annual billings tenfold . . . from $70,000 to $700,000!

Susan owns a human resources consulting company. She wanted to grow by increasing her visibility with companies with 25 to 200 employees who might need the products and services her company offers, such as group health care, 401(k) plans, and the like. Susan's solution was to form a Smart-Match Alliance with a large professional association. She offered to deliver free TeleForums on human resources-related topics to member companies and to write articles for their association newsletter. In exchange, she received high visibility among association members.

As a result of this high visibility, this SmartMatch Alliance produced 400 new clients for Susan among association members. The Association itself became one of Susan's clients, asking her to design a 401(k) program for its members. The alliance led to an increase in revenue of $500,000 for the association and $150,000 for Susan's company.

The Association was able to offer members a new long-distance training tool using TeleForums, and Susan added new companies to her client roster . . . a win-win combination.

 ## BREAKING AWAY

SmartMatch Alliances represent a new way of thinking about your business, its potential, and your approach to business-building, whether you intend to grow in your existing markets or expand into new territories.

For this reason, your greatest challenge isn't changing your business or your leadership style. It's changing your mind, shedding success-stalling, go-it-alone habits and paradigms in favor of new, synergistic, cooperative—and fun!— business-building strategies.

This process of *un*learning and cultivating new levels of awareness of the factors, big and small, that influence your success may feel unfamiliar and strange at first, but it's critical to reaching the next level of success and growth through SmartMatch Alliances. The quickest way to make room for new, empowering, and growth-enhancing ideas is to deliberately and systematically ditch some of the old, disempowering ways that no longer work, particularly those that are deeply ingrained, traditional ways of thinking and operating as business professionals.

In the next section, we begin to describe the step-by-step SmartMatch Alliance process for using strategic alliances to expand your horizons and build your business, and it begins, not surprisingly, with a step we call **Think Big** on page 17.

two

SmartMatch Alliances . . . Step by Step

"When he took the time to help the man up the mountain,
lo, he scaled it himself."

—UNKNOWN

For many years, information was hard to find, often involving trips to the library, searches through scores of books, records, microfiche (remember microfiche?!), and more. If you had the stamina and patience to cull through these resources and emerge from the library stacks hunched over and squinting, you deserved giant kudos.

But, of course, the world has changed. Today, pure information is everywhere. Pick a search engine, enter a word or phrase, and 64,598 results pop up in front of you on your computer screen. In itself, information provokes a well-deserved, eyes-to-the-ceiling, "Big deeeal!" from just about anyone.

Answers—fast responses to key questions—elevate pure information to the next level of power and value. The questions that produce answers are fact-based . . .

How much will it cost? What quantities are we likely to sell in Europe? If we moved production offshore, would we realize significant economies? How is the public likely to respond to our website? What's my aggressive competition doing? Who's got a similar product or service? How can I find the perfect vendor—a zillion miles away?

Answers keep businesses moving forward with speed and agility.

Solutions are the next—and perhaps highest—level. Solutions are business intelligence . . . answers in action. The questions that produce solutions are action-based . . .

How do we reduce costs? What can we do to increase the quantities we sell to clients and customers . . . past, present, and future—wherever they are? How can we reach more high-potential prospects? How do we gracefully increase our rates and prices? What steps can we take to enhance the quality and variety of what we produce and sell?

Solutions propel businesses, catapulting them forward and upward too.

Today—and for the foreseeable (and unforeseeable!) future—solutions, or answers in action, wield the real power. Essentially, what can you *do* with what you know? How can you organize and manage the information you have to make it work for you? What types of clever connections can you make? What people, products, and services can you put together? Where will imagination and intuition lead you?

The real edge in business today is in finding unique ways to apply what you know . . . to leverage your knowledge, expertise, and business relationships for growth and success.

This means you are sitting on a gold mine! Taken together, your base of clients along with your ideas, knowledge, and expertise have the power to propel your business and your career forward and upward . . . *when*—and this is key—*when and only when you know the steps to take.*

The steps, quite simply, are the phases of SmartMatch Alliance building, a process we call the **SmartMatch Cycle of Success**©, shown here.

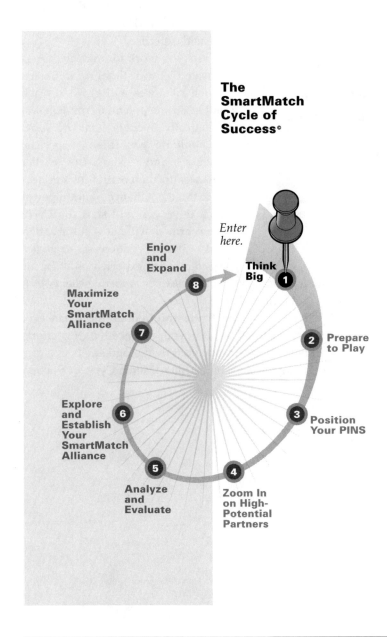

The SmartMatch Cycle of Success°

Enter here.

Think Big 1

Enjoy and Expand 8

Maximize Your SmartMatch Alliance 7

Explore and Establish Your SmartMatch Alliance 6

Analyze and Evaluate 5

Zoom In on High-Potential Partners 4

Position Your PINS 3

Prepare to Play 2

When you use the eight steps in the **SmartMatch Cycle of Success** in sequence, you build strong strategic alliances, each a power-packed sales and marketing strategy for you and your company. This means you will wake up the sleeping giant in your base of clients, in your ideas, your marketing niche, and your knowledge and expertise.

An Important Note from the Coaches

Resist the temptation to cut corners or skip steps in the **SmartMatch Cycle of Success**. Maximize the effectiveness and power of your SmartMatch Alliances by working carefully through each step in succession.

As you work through the **Cycle** repeatedly over time, your Smart-Match Alliances will grow in reach and in upside potential. You will systematically leverage what you know by applying your ideas, expertise, resources, and learnings from earlier alliances to the creation of the next SmartMatch Alliance—and the next. Each time, you will start the **Cycle** anew armed with new information and powerful success strategies based on your experiences and your goals for expanding your businesses by attracting clients, customers, and future alliance partners.

We'll reference the **Cycle** throughout the balance of *SmartMatch Alliances*. Use it in your alliance-building efforts as a handy tool for watching your own progress.

Let's take the steps in the **SmartMatch Cycle of Success** one by one.

Step 1
Think Big

T he ancient Greeks had no convenient system of notation or simple way of writing very large numbers. Archimedes, perhaps the greatest mathematician of all time, saw this as a severe barrier to thinking big, so he invented a system of numbers based on the Greek "myriad," or 10,000. In "The Sand Treatise" he set forth the concept of a "myriad of myriads" and multiplied these numbers by themselves a myriad times—and again—until he reached a huge number that we would express as a 1 followed by 80 million billion zeros.

This, said Archimedes, "is a quite adequate number."

What do you need to create to think this big?

Begin with an intensive session of personal and business <u>un</u>learning.

Starting today—right now—we want you to begin to think in new ways:

- away from "go it alone" and toward joyful collaboration with like-minded colleagues

- away from one dimension ("My success is directly proportional to my investment of blood, sweat, and tears . . .") and toward a matrix of ideas and professional relationships that produces exponential success

- away from "in-person as often as possible" and toward "as virtual as possible," drawing on the best resources, minds, ideas, products, services, and more . . . regardless of where they're located around the globe

- away from "risk averse" and toward "risk-free experimentation with new ideas"

Let's take these one by one.

Away from "go it alone" and toward joyful collaboration with like-minded colleagues . . .

You no longer have to feel alone. We promise you can find people with influence, inspiration, and exposure out there ready and willing to support your goals and perhaps become your alliance partners. They have the knowledge, information, contacts, marketing engines, and ideas you need. And they would welcome an alliance as much as you would. In fact, they will soon want to get to know you and your business, in a balanced and mutually beneficial way. There will be no uncomfortably vague quid pro quo because your Exchange of Value or EOV (you'll find much more on EOVs starting on page 80) will be clearly identified.

"Loyalty to a petrified opinion never yet broke a chain or freed a human soul."
—Mark Twain, American author

Away from one dimension and toward a matrix of ideas and professional relationships that produces exponential success . . .

You must expand your thinking beyond one dimension ("I must promote," "I must scramble for work," "I must struggle to close sales") to multi-dimensional approaches such as cause and effect, leverage, strength in numbers, a whole greater than the sum of its parts, and synergy).

Away from "in-person as often as possible" and toward "as virtual as possible" . . .

Whether you provide a product or a service, your time is money! In-person appearances are one of the most expensive ways to conduct business because they cost you twice: the implicit value of your time (the cost of your salary and benefits to be there) and the opportunity cost of not being able to use that time to accomplish something else that would bring a higher return.

Here's an example of what we mean. Your drive to work takes 45 minutes, but you've recently discovered an alternate route that will save you 15 minutes each way. That's a half hour a day, 2½ hours each week, 10 hours a month, 120 hours a year, three full 40-hour work weeks of time that you can reclaim as yours. Would you change your route? Of course you would! Because you intuitively know that your time is valuable. And because it makes no sense to spend time in ways that you don't value.

From this day forward, never let yourself say, "Well, all I spent was my own time" or "At least it cost me nothing to find that out." Even if you spent no out-of-pocket money, you spent precious time, and that translates into money. Every time you appeared in person to negotiate a deal, you spent money.

Value your time as a precious commodity!

Think back once more to Archimedes who, in about 240 A.D. said (more or less), "Give me a lever long enough and a place to stand, and I will move the earth." He was excited to have found proofs of the mathematical laws of the lever, an implement that enables a person to exert little effort to achieve a disproportionately large result.

Technology is today's version of the very long lever . . . the technology we use to run global businesses from virtual offices, build alliances with people from around the world, and reach markets everywhere. Now, that's leverage!

Away from "risk averse" and toward "risk-free experimentation with new ideas" . . .

Risk can be a scary word in business. We've learned to steer clear of the just-too-good-to-be-true ventures, the get-rich-quick schemes, and smoke-and-mirrors opportunities. Sometimes the greatest risk is doing nothing, repeating the same failing strategies, staying with the same markets or products, even keeping customers who would be served better by someone else. We stay put and then wonder why success eludes us. We are living, according to Albert Einstein, the very definition of insanity, which, said Einstein, is the practice of "doing the same thing over and over again and expecting a different result."

Alliances are not high-risk ventures, but rather intelligent experiments with the new and untried. Of course, not all alliances produce results. But the **SmartMatch Cycle of Success** enables you to craft each alliance so that even the least favorable outcomes don't constitute failure, but rather valuable lessons you apply to building your next SmartMatch Alliance . . . and the next.

With alliance-building experience, you begin to trust yourself and your expertise. You emerge smarter, stronger, and more knowledgeable for next time.

Plan? Absolutely. Just don't live there.

Ever wish you had a dime for every time you've heard the advice to write down your goals: "Every dream requires a plan," "If you can dream it, you can do it," "A goal is a dream with a deadline," "When you fail to plan, you plan to fail"?

These are galvanizing statements, and surely it's essential to have a destination for yourself and your company. Goals are critical for thinking big, for envisioning and then building a life of unabashed passion, fun, fulfillment, and sheer joy. In fact, we advise our coaching clients to pull out the stops and create what we call Googol Goals. "Googol" is a mathematical word coined by American mathematician Edward Kassner that refers to a very, very large number. We want you to set Googol Goals that get you out of bed in the morning and keep your juices flowing all day.

"Ah, but a man's reach should exceed his grasp, or what's a heaven for?"
—Robert Browning,
19th century English poet

So goals, yes, definitely. A plan? Gotta have it. But, BUT . . . don't be so busy dreaming and planning that you get nothing done. We call this the "Ready . . . Aim . . . Aim . . . Aim . . . " approach to success . . . or failure!

We've designed an exercise we use with our coaching clients to take them beyond static goal setting into the dynamic and vivid imaginings of individuals and businesses embarking on their SmartMatch Alliance journey.

Take out your *Alliance Journal.* On a fresh, clean page, write down this sentence stem:

I wish _____

Create a minimum of five responses. Here are some examples to guide your thinking:

- I wish *my résumé service were featured on monster.com.*
- I wish *every new subscriber to the* Wall Street Journal *received my book on leadership.*
- I wish *my CPA firm were recommended by every attorney in town.*

- I wish *every Happy Meal® came with my toy cartoon characters.*

- I wish *every Lexus® buyer received a brochure featuring my website and my winery.*

- I wish *my high-speed Internet connections were built into every new apartment community.*

- I wish *my software products were on every computer desktop.*

These "I wish" ideas are very important! Keep them nearby as we work through the balance of the SmartMatch Alliance building process.

Do your genius work every day.

"The mass of men lead lives of quiet desperation," wrote Thoreau, surely one of the most influential and widely-read figures in American thought and literature. Thoreau's words beautifully capture the strain we so often hear in the voices of many of our coaching clients around the world, whether they are hard-charging entrepreneurs or dynamic corporate executives.

When we first begin working with our clients, we find them struggling with cash flow, struggling to stay competitive in an increasingly global economy, struggling to balance business, life, and family. In larger companies, our new clients may be struggling to make their budgets, struggling to stay employed, struggling to work with a manager who doesn't like them, or struggling to motivate a team that doesn't want to work together.

"You need to stop struggling and begin to do more of your genius work," we advise.

The response is often a confused, "My what?"

"Your genius work," we explain. "Genius work is the highest and best use of your time. When you do your genius work—the activities that produce the greatest results in the shortest period of time for you—the struggle ends . . . fast."

What this means is that your genius work is, by definition, your greatest leverage.

Your genius work commands your full attention. It focuses your energy on the activities and the action steps that deliver high-impact results. Genius work is pure joy . . . love in motion. Your genius work is healthy, engaging, and uplifting, and it causes you to draw positive events and people to you. When you're engrossed in your genius work, time stops. You can easily skip a meal and not realize it. You're happy and full of ideas.

And your genius work can only be done by you.

If you are a business owner, your genius work may include activities like:

- delivering a large sales presentation
- leading an international meeting
- planning business strategy for the year
- speaking at a large trade show or industry event
- contacting and meeting with a new strategic alliance partner
- expanding a strategic alliance

If you are a business leader in a large organization, your genius work may include activities like:

- conducting an important interview to hire a new superstar employee
- negotiating with a key vendor
- developing a marketing strategy for a product launch
- preparing and delivering a presentation to your board of directors
- contacting and meeting with a new strategic alliance partner
- expanding a strategic alliance

Your **Genius Work**

It's time to identify *your* genius work, so take out your *Alliance Journal.* On a fresh, clean page, write down this question:

What three areas of focus and corresponding activities would constitute the best and most valuable use of my time today?

Refer back to the lists above to guide your thinking.

On another page of your *Alliance Journal,* record all your activities in 15-minute increments during each day of a five-day work week.

Next, circle the time spent in the three areas of focus you identified as your genius work for the day, the highest and best use of your time.

Take a moment to reflect on your results. If you're like nearly every one of our coaching clients at the start of our working together, you'll find you're spending the least amount of time on your most significant genius work.

Your next step is to label your activities in those 15-minute increments in two categories: a "Must-be-done" list and a "Delegate" list.

Label as "Must-be-done" the activities and projects that require your attention today but could actually be completed by someone else if you spent 30 to 90 minutes showing this person the necessary steps and desired outcomes. For instance, your "Must-be-done" list might include invoicing clients, planning your trade show booth theme, or conducting Internet research on a potential alliance partner.

Investing 30 to 90 minutes of your time to explain the processes and required outcomes needed to handle activities on your "Must-be-done" list enables you to confidently pass on these important tasks—forever—to a competent, well-trained person, giving you more time to spend on your genius work.

Our coaching clients' "Must-be-done" lists are always very long, and we devote lots of time during our weekly coaching calls helping to remove every activity and project on their "Must-be-done" list in order to free up 10 to 20 hours of their time each week. It works! In fact, some of our clients who hadn't taken time off in years are now enjoying monthly vacations on sandy beaches. Others are semi-retired at 45, and still others are spending more time with their families . . . as they always wanted to.

Label as "Delegate" those activities and projects that can be completed quickly and require only 30 to 60 *seconds* of explanation. For example, your assistant can make copies of a presentation you'll be delivering to a potential alliance partner, your sales director can generate and deliver sales reports at your next executive meeting, and a team member can send out your E-newsletter. These are all one-step requests that can be easily delegated to members of your team.

When you identify your genius work and clear the way for it to take up as large a percentage of your time as possible, you become a more efficient, prosperous person and business . . . and a more powerful and appealing alliance partner at the same time.

By the way, starting today, you can add SmartMatch Alliance building to the activities that comprise your genius work!

Assess your alliance-ability.

The inimitable Groucho Marx once said, "I'd never join a club that would have me as a member." We use a variation of Groucho's quip to get deeper into the process of thinking through strategic alliances with our coaching clients. It's a process of self-assessment, of taking stock if you will, that ultimately asks the question: "Are you someone you'd like to partner with?"

Take some time now to answer the following questions:

Reminder

Photocopy the following form and insert it into your *Alliance Journal* before beginning. Keeping a clean original will permit you to use the SmartMatch Alliance worksheets many times!

ALLIANCE-ABILITY CHECKLIST©

Your Reputation and Skills   **Yes!**

1. Do you have a well-earned reputation for succeeding? ☐

2. Do you have a reputation for being trustworthy in
   your business dealings? ☐

3. Do you have a sense of what a win-win relationship
   looks and feels like? ☐

4. Are you visible within your profession, industry,
   niches, and specialty? ☐

Your Communication

5. Do you communicate effectively with others—
   verbally, in writing, through E-mail? ☐

6. Have you mastered the art of listening between the lines
   for important information and solid opportunities?
   Can you hear what is not said as well as what is said? ☐

7. Can you say, "Yesssss!"? (And can you say, "No thanks!"?) ☐

8. Do you reply to phone calls, faxes, and E-mails
   within 24 hours? ☐

Your Readiness Level

9. Are you ready to take your business and/or career
   to the next level? ☐

10. Are you ready to think outside the box? ☐

11. Do you want to make more money? ☐

12. Are you flexible and open to new ideas? ☐

continued

Your Standards

13. Are you surrounded by a team of superstars? ☐

14. Do your written materials have a world-class image? ☐

15. When something goes wrong, do you fix it quickly? ☐

16. Do you learn from your mistakes? ☐

17. Do you keep your word? ☐

You

18. Will an alliance with you be fun and easy? ☐

19. Do you believe in the power of alliances? ☐

20. Do you have the tenacity to pursue an alliance you believe in? ☐

21. Do you have the patience to see the alliance commitment through to the end? ☐

Now, count your Yeses . . .

18 to 21:

You are absolutely alliance-able! What are you waiting for?!

12 to 17:

You've got some work to do. Review the principles and success tips in **Step 1: Think Big** as well as those that follow in **Step 2: Prepare to Play.** Be certain you're practicing the principles and strategies in these sections before attempting to form a SmartMatch Alliance.

Complete the *Alliance-Ability Checklist* again after three to six months.

0 to 11:

You're *not* yet prepared for alliances! You need to take a "back to basics" approach to building your business and

An Important Note from the Coaches

You *must* honestly assess your alliance-ability before setting out to build SmartMatch Alliances. We know from experience with many of our coaching clients that the specific questions in the *Alliance-Ability Checklist* are a highly telling means of determining whether a person or a company is truly ready to become involved in the sort of give and take required of a successful alliance relationship.

Unless you're alliance-able, at best, your alliance won't produce the results you're after. At worst, it may fail altogether, costing you in many ways: you will have lost an alliance partner—probably permanently, the potential benefits and exposure the alliance was going to deliver for you and your company, and the time and other resources you invested in what became an unproductive alliance. Not a pretty picture!

So, take your time and be certain you've got alliance-ability. Your improved outcomes will more than make up for the advance work required to ensure you're ready, willing, and able to capitalize on the right alliance opportunities at the right time.

career. Rethink essential processes and decision points and begin to shape your business or career around the foundational success principles outlined in this book, including the essential marketing and communication practices and business-building strategies.

Complete the *Alliance-Ability Checklist* again after six months to a year.

 SUMMING UP

There's a word that neatly sums up the shift in your mindset required to "think big." It's *awakening*. Awakening to the fact that you and your company are not alone: other professionals out there have a real interest in your success—because they have a passion for their own success.

"To see the World in a grain of Sand
And Heaven in a wild Flower Hold
Infinity in the palm of your hand
And Eternity in an hour."
—William Blake,
19th century English poet

Awakening to the matrix of possibilities, to the value of your time, and to the power of intelligent experiments.

As you systematically think big and raise the bar for yourself and your business, you prepare yourself to hear opportunity's knock. Your next step is to be certain you're ready to open the door . . . and **Prepare to Play.**

A Cautionary Tale: Don't Spend Too Much Time Hunting Elephants

Here's an example of what can happen when you're looking to bag "the big one."

Who's Who: Coaching Success and a major U.S.-based membership association with more than 10 million members considered the possibilities of a SmartMatch Alliance.

The Goals: The association wanted to use the Coaching Success Tele-Forum model for distance learning. In turn, we saw tremendous potential for leverage, given the size of the association's membership.

The SmartMatch Alliance Breaker: It was difficult to get agreement on the alliance internally to the association because of the many levels of approval inherent in a large, hierarchical organization. Also, as is often the case in large organizations, the association suffered from what we call the "not-invented-here" syndrome, which can make it tough to introduce innovative ideas and strategies created by "outside" companies and vendors.

The Win-Win: Rather than enter into an alliance with the association, we delivered advanced training on TeleForums on a fee-for-services basis.

The Takeaway: Giant alliances can take years and years to bear fruit. Remember to continue the search for small and medium-sized alliances. They can be created quickly, and they work! Don't get so caught up in chasing the big one that you miss the smaller, solid, and highly profitable strategic alliances right in front of you!

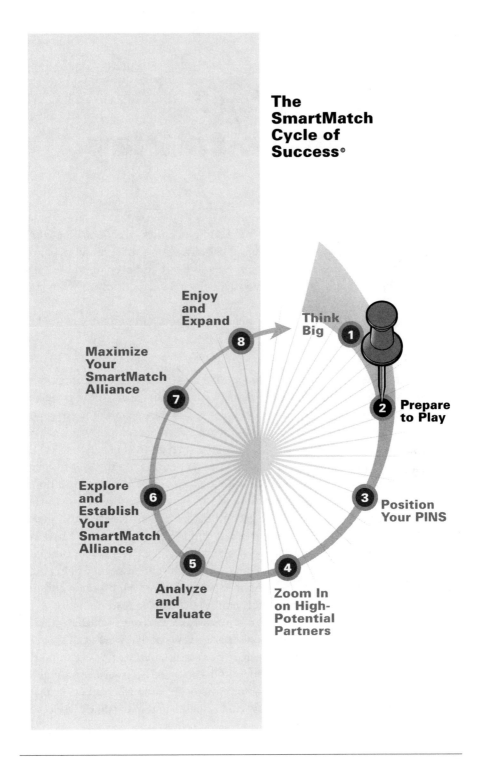

The
SmartMatch
Cycle of
Success©

Enjoy
and
Expand

Think
Big ❶

❽

Maximize
Your
SmartMatch
Alliance

❼

❷ Prepare
to Play

Explore
and
Establish
Your
SmartMatch
Alliance

❻

❸ Position
Your PINS

❺

❹

Analyze
and
Evaluate

Zoom In
on High-
Potential
Partners

Step 2
Prepare to Play

"Luck is the residue of design," said Branch Rickey, general manager of the Dodgers in the '40s and '50s. The point to be made is: chance favors the ready. You must open your mind and heart and prepare to capitalize on the best alliance opportunities as you actively and energetically draw them to you at a faster and faster rate.

What actions will jumpstart your alliance readiness and prepare you to play?

Develop readiness habits.

Adopt the attitude—and more important, the habits—of readiness. Readiness habits take you beyond the due diligence of running your business (the "ABCs" of making sure you're offering a product or service of value to your target market, keeping your sales promotion efforts and materials sharp, staying competitive in your product/service packaging and pricing, maintaining an up-to-date database, etc.).

Readiness habits enable you to recognize unplanned opportunities, make nonlinear connections, take a leap of faith based on your instincts, make timely adjustments in your business plans, look for the new, the different, the untried, and take pioneering steps onto new ground before anyone else. All this means your readiness habits ensure that you're not blindsided by change or lured into believing that your business, market, colleagues, centers of influence, or processes are out of reach of the next downturn or economic shift because they help you to realize that—for better or worse—everything changes. Indeed, it's not a question of whether things will change but when, and . . . will you be ready?

We live in a world in which Jeff Bezos' upstart amazon.com—which became an enormous online bookstore . . . what a pioneering concept that was!—can show up out of nowhere and gain huge market share from an established bricks and mortar chain like Barnes & Noble. One in which AOL can build a subscriber base in the tens of millions that eclipses the behemoth Microsoft®, and Michael Dell can cut classes to build PCs in his garage—how cool is that?—and make quick work of no less a business icon than IBM in a matter of years. A world in which an E-trade can come along and shake a venerable institution like Merrill Lynch, causing a reorganization of massive proportions. One in which managers of classified advertising departments in traditional newspapers stood like deer in the headlights while employers and job hunters alike turned to monster.com and headhunter.net in droves.

> *"The only way to make sense out of change is to plunge into it, move with it, and join the dance."*
> —*Alan Watts,*
> *Author and lecturer on Zen philosophy*

What all of these examples tell us is that while technology has played a huge role in leveling the playing field and challenging the law of "size = leverage," the need to preserve the status quo and the fear of change have also had roles to play. The need to protect existing business models can make large companies vulnerable because it saps their creative energy and causes them to take their eyes off the ball. The result: missed opportunities, lack of innovation, and at best, low-impact responses to market forces.

These examples also tell us that larger companies have begun to see the high price they pay for sticking with old paradigms and operating models. As this clarity grows, companies become increasingly receptive to the right alliances with the right partners, whether these partners are large, small, or somewhere in between.

The following readiness habits—many of which are simply good business—will serve you well no matter who you are or what level of opportunity and success you're after:

- Make the time to read everything you can lay your hands on about trends and developments in your current and target PINS, once again, your profession, industry, niche, and specialties. How are other businesses handling the same competitive and business pressures you're facing? New opportunities? New threats? What does this suggest about the ways you may need to respond? Increase or decrease staff? Invest in new technologies? Relocate? What impact will these events and changes have on your goals, your alliances, and your future?

Subscribe to the publications that serve your PINS. In addition, consider subscribing to publications like *Wired, Inc., Fast Company, Money, Adweek, Selling Power, ComputerWorld, Fortune,* and others that offer information which will help you stay in touch with local, state, regional, and national business, technology, and demographic trends.

- Watch for the changes that are shaping the future of your industry, the marketplace, and the world of business. Notice cause and effect . . . what are the strategies today that yield high rewards? Who's succeeding today and why? For instance, read and review the *Inc. 500.* Ask yourself why companies like Morningstar, Jamba Juice, CWS Corporate Leasing, and Navigator Systems have been listed multiple times.

- As we advise our coaching clients, be a lifelong learner. Keep your skills, resources, and expertise current. The extent of your ability to adapt to and capitalize on opportunities is in direct proportion to your efforts to stay up-to-date in your area of expertise, targeted niches, and specialties. Consider investing the time and money to upgrade your professional certifications as this says to your peers and colleagues that you are serious about your business, profession, or career. Expand your learning area well beyond the traditional media of classroom, seminar, and formal training. Investigate opportunities for distance learning—by computer, by telephone, by video conference, or any combination of these. Contact seminar companies who deliver programs aimed at advancing your specific business or personal skills in a short amount of time and with minimal investment.

Start each year by selecting the industry or professional seminars and trade shows you will be attending. Then plan, schedule, and set an annual budget for meetings and education. Now look at your calendar and reserve the time and dates you are going to schedule for the professional and personal learning that will best serve you. As a rule of thumb, consider budgeting at least $50 to $150 per month for your continued education. This small investment today will pay large dividends in the near and distant future.

- Search the Internet for companies with websites that serve your PINS and register for their E-newsletters, subscribe to their E-mail discussion lists, and participate in live and interactive telephone conference calls, like TeleForums (see page 63 for a concise definition and strategies for hosting TeleForums), to experience an engaging and valuable form of distance learning.

- Watch for mergers, acquisitions, partnerships, new allegiances, and alliances. Who's partnering with whom? What cooperative ventures are underway? Have businesses or divisions been bought or sold?

- Listen to tapes and CDs on change readiness, goal-setting, personal effectiveness, accountability, and productivity enhancements. Fill your mind with positive thoughts about change and opportunity.

- Continue to master the technology that powers your industry and your profession. Above all, customize your technology so it serves you well.

Here's an activity that will get you excited about lifelong learning and other readiness habits. Take out your *Alliance Journal*. On a fresh, clean page, provide at least three sets of phrases to complete this sentence:

Learning _____ will help me _____ so I'll be ready to _____ when the alliance opportunity arises.

This exercise may yield some of the following activities:

- take a PowerPoint® course
- join a speakers' forum such as Toastmasters
- participate on the board of a non-profit organization
- learn a new language
- take a speedreading course
- learn powerful negotiation skills

Keep your responses close at hand as you expand your horizons . . . and your business. Your answers will help inspire your readiness habits by encouraging you to rise to the challenge of lifelong growth and learning and by keeping what's at stake squarely in front of you as it relates to building SmartMatch Alliances.

Maximize your use of technology.

In the world of SmartMatch Alliances, size doesn't matter. An alliance between a large and a small partner can be just as successful as one between two small partners. And alliances among small local companies will enable you to compete with larger regional, national, or even international companies.

For this kind of alliance leverage we credit today's ultra-swift, user-friendly computers, easy Internet access and ubiquitous E-mail capabilities. Through easy access and ease of use, these technologies have leveled the business playing field. In the minds of your potential alliance partners, you can exhibit the characteristics and qualities of a small, medium, or large company—or a conglomerate. When you combine a good-looking, effective website, perhaps an information-packed E-newsletter, and a team of people (whether they are in one location or dispersed around the world) interested in providing superior quality and service, the size of your company is invisible . . . and irrelevant.

Technology has forever changed the world of work and the paradigm of "size = leverage." Power and leverage have shifted. Today, the win goes to the team capable of delivering superior performance—fast—be it large, small, or just about anything in between.

And though technology with lots of "bells and whistles" is definitely not prerequisite to forming SmartMatch Alliances, it gives you fast access to information, the ability to communicate rapidly, and the power to react quickly and capitalize on emerging alliance opportunities. Technology also has the potential to make you much more attractive to a potential alliance partner. The more contacts, information access, exposure, creative ideas, and overall capabilities you bring to the alliance table, so to speak, the more alliance-ability you have. More on this later.

For these reasons, we suggest tooling up with whatever you need that will help you build your business into an enterprise that's lean, sharp, and fast on its feet. We've found that when it comes to technology, some people are much further ahead than others, so if you're not tech-savvy, consider getting the help you need from experts.

Other suggestions:

- Have a speedy, reliable, and convenient Internet connection, web browser, and E-mail system. Take the time to familiarize yourself with the features and functions of each to maximize their value to you. Learn and master the specific software used by your company. Learn the shortcuts for creating professional-looking correspondence, presentations, and proposals.

- Plan for tomorrow. Maintain a level of sophistication in your technology aimed at serving today's best clients and customers and the clients and customers of tomorrow . . . not yesterday.

- Maximize your use of the Internet to expand your networking, customer service, marketing, research, and career planning. Create an E-newsletter and build your subscriber list (by permission only, of course!).

Use software that will manage your subscriber list and send out your E-newsletter—seamlessly.

- Understand and practice "Netiquette." Be concise and positive in your E-mails. Do not send unsolicited E-mail. Respect the privacy of the people and businesses in your E-mail database . . . which means do not share their names and addresses with other marketers.

- Become an expert user of a database management system or contact management software. Use it to gather and analyze strategic information about your sales and marketing efforts.

Be ready for inspiration . . . whenever it hits.

Many of the best ideas and solutions come to us when we least expect them . . . while stepping out of the office building for a breath of fresh air, grocery shopping, showering, sitting in traffic, weeding the garden, staring into space over a cup of coffee, or driving to the golf course.

There we are, going about our business, when suddenly— aha! A palm slap to the head accompanied by "Why didn't I think of that alliance idea before?"

We've all had this experience. Our minds are at ease during non-working times or rote activities. We're essentially on automatic pilot. These are clearly times of great alliance inspiration.

Back once more to our friend Archimedes.

Many people know the story of Archimedes running naked through the streets of Syracuse crying, "Eureka! Eureka!!" ("I have found it! I have found it!!") Archimedes was delirious with the excitement of discovery: he had just hit upon what was to become the basic law of hydraulic engineering.

"The eye sees a great many things, but the average brain records very few of them."

—Thomas Edison, American inventor and entrepreneur

Archimedes had been asked by the king to do some detective work to determine whether the court crown maker had substituted silver for gold in the king's new crown. While taking a bath,

Tuning in to Tomorrow

Here's an example of how an automotive magazine and a radio station joined forces to increase ad revenues.

Who's Who: Jonathan is the publisher of an automotive magazine and a Coaching Success client. He approached a radio station whose demographics matched those of this readers.

The Goals: Jonathan wanted to gain exposure to his target market by creating his own radio show that would showcase experts on automotive topics. The radio station wanted to sell more air time and more ads, and to create a magazine/radio package for its sales force.

The EOV: For a negotiated and reduced fee, Jonathan purchased a 60-minute time slot for a weekly show. In exchange, the radio station was able to include Jonathan's magazine in its sales package.

The Win-Win: In addition to selling air time, the radio station sold new advertisers drawn by Jonathan's show and his magazine. The advertising revenue for Jonathan's publication also increased substantially because of the package of the radio show and the magazine and the increased exposure the magazine received on air. Both partners increased their revenues significantly.

The Takeaway: Forming an alliance with a radio station can increase your profitability and visibility with very little money changing hands.

Archimedes noticed his own weight in water spilling over the edge of the tub and realized that a solid immersed in liquid loses as much weight as the weight of the water it pushes aside. He was later able to weigh amounts of silver and the gold equal to the weight of the crown . . . and catch the court crown maker at his crime.

Ernest Hemingway spent many hours at the Musee du Luxembourg viewing works of impressionist art. In an

An Important Note from the Coaches

In **Step 3: Position Your PINS,** we begin to show you how to build a specific SmartMatch Alliance. We've included a number of worksheets and checklists that will help you construct your first SmartMatch Alliance. We strongly encourage you to complete these worksheets, work through each of the checklists, and respond to the questions and prompts.

We want to pause here to underscore the importance of the experiential learning these exercises provide. When you complete each step of the Smart-Match Alliance process in its proper sequence, you become more and more engaged on an experiential level, a process that will help you tremendously in your efforts to build strong, valuable strategic alliances and to make this powerful tool a permanent part of your business-building toolbox.

Keep an *Alliance Journal* for ongoing, easy reference (which can be purchased and downloaded at our website www.coachingsuccess.com). Since you'll uncover new success strategies in the process of building each Smart-Match Alliance, you'll benefit from having a place to record and store lessons, notes, and ideas that will help you build better (more powerful, more profitable . . . and more fun!) alliances in the future.

As you continue your SmartMatch Alliance journey, remember the Native American saying: "I *see*, and I forget. I *hear*, and I remember. I *do* and I understand." Your mind cannot forget what your hands create. Give yourself the gift of this opportunity.

interview with the *Paris Review*, he was asked to name the literary figures who inspired him. Hemingway responded with a list that included not only writers, but Cezanne, van Gogh, and Mozart. As he put it, the works of these artists helped him learn "to see, to hear, to feel and not feel, and to write." "I learn as much from painters about how to write as from writers," he explained.

Be ready for alliance inspiration to hit in unlikely places and at unexpected moments. Carry your *Alliance Journal* with you everywhere and quickly jot down new ideas. Note any connections about opportunities to capitalize on shifts in your business or PINS. Carry a metaphorical magnifying glass to see the deep details and a telescope to increase your vision and reach.

The steps and strategies included in **Prepare to Play** may be new to you, but we can tell you that they do work, and that they can be learned. The magic ingredient is simple to acquire—it's the commitment to take the action steps that catapult your result above that of the merely theoretical absorber. Don't be a sponge; be a rocket ship! And . . . to add yet another metaphor to this mixed bag . . . think of this investment in "getting ready" as a process of planting seeds that will germinate into healthy, powerful SmartMatch Alliances.

It's time now to begin planning your SmartMatch Alliances . . . and to **Position your PINS.**

The SmartMatch Cycle of Success©

Enjoy and Expand

Think Big **1**

Maximize Your SmartMatch Alliance **7**

8

2 Prepare to Play

Explore and Establish Your SmartMatch Alliance **6**

3 Position Your PINS

5

4

Analyze and Evaluate

Zoom In on High-Potential Partners

Step 3 ———
Position Your PINS

Y ou've begun to see the world in different terms. You've done some mental and business "housecleaning" and replaced old habits with new, empowering ones. It's time to begin thinking in specific alliance-building terms.

Your next step is to identify potential alliance partners and also to help them identify you by making yourself visible to them.

Questions immediately come to your mind:

- "How, when, and where do alliance partners typically find each other?"
- "How will I know a potential alliance partner when I see one?"
- "Are there ways to make myself and my company not just visible, but a standout?"

To answer these and many other questions, we use a method we call PINS, which refers to the practice of making yourself known as an expert resource and a major player to the people and businesses who share your current and target profession, industry, niches, and specialties.

Your *current* PINS are the Profession, Industry, Niches, and Specialties in which you conduct business today.

Your *target* PINS are the Profession, Industry, Niches, and Specialties in which you'd like to conduct business.

Example: a CPA (profession) with concentrated expertise in the accounting and financial intricacies of software companies (industry, niche) and a special aptitude in profitability consulting for start-up businesses (specialty).

Focusing your alliance-building efforts on your current and target PINS enables you to laser in on the highest potential alliance partners. (It's also one of the reasons we so strongly encourage you to follow the steps in **The SmartMatch Cycle of Success** in sequence!) Once you put the PINS strategy in place, you're guaranteed to be in the right place at the right time. You're positioned so effectively that you become a magnet for alliance partners. Your alliance-building energy is concentrated only in the most promising areas, and your results reflect this intensity of focus.

When you position your PINS, your alliance-building efforts are streamlined, efficient, and effective . . . all of which are critical to realizing the power, leverage, and exponential growth strategic alliances are capable of producing.

For these reasons, the PINS approach is the essence of effortless marketing, and all of the SmartMatch Alliance building process cascades from it.

Identify your current and target PINS.

Take out your *Alliance Journal*. On a clean page, write down descriptions of your *current* PINS . . . the profession(s), industry(ies), niche(s), and specialty(ies) in which your business operates today.

Next, identify your *target* PINS. To do so, consider where you'd like you and your company to be in the next three to five years. Take out your *Alliance Journal* and review your "I wish" list. What did the "I wish" activity reveal about the

Niches and Specialties

A niche is like a market segment, e.g., certain types of clients or customers. Here are some examples of niches: entrepreneurs, dentists, high-tech manufacturers, teachers, parents, and people in career transition.

A niche is WHO you're focusing on.

Your specialty is a set of skills or proficiencies that can be used across many professions, industries, and niches.

A specialty is WHAT you're good at doing or making or teaching or selling.

professions, industries, niches, and specialties you'd like to pursue in the future?

As an example, let's say that your "I wish" list included a statement like:

> "I wish *my Dental Practice Building Workbooks were standard training for every dental office worker nationwide.*"

You'd then think about individuals and businesses you could create an alliance with that would put your *Workbooks* in the hands of every dental practice in the country. If you were based in the U.S., you'd reach out for the president and/or meeting coordinator of the American Dental Association and offer to speak for free at their annual meeting in Washington, D.C., as long as your materials were available for sale in the back of the meeting room. You'd contact the editor of *Dental Success* magazine and offer to write free articles in exchange for having your byline include a mention of your *Workbook* and your website address.

You see, your "I wish" list has helped you identify your target PINS, and you're now going full steam ahead!

In your efforts to identify your target PINS, you might also consider who your clients, customers, and prospects of the future will be. More specifically, where will the demand for your products, services, and expertise be most intense in the next three to five years? Is your profession or industry becoming more automated? If you're a meeting-planning service, for instance, are you on top of the trend in your industry toward full automation of the meeting-planning process within corporations? Did you know that these organizations are purchasing complex software packages that take all the guesswork and complex logistics out of planning their sales and incentive meetings? How can you position your PINS to capitalize on this trend?

How are your clients' and customers' needs, wants, and preferences already changing—perhaps in ways even they don't yet see? Consider the vinyl record business, an industry valued in the hundreds of millions, if not billions, that was all but wiped out in a period of a few years, replaced by compact disk technology. Before CDs and CD players were widely available, consumers didn't know they'd prefer the sound, convenience, and durability of CDs over vinyl records, but of course they did! What will your clients, customers, and prospects want in the coming years that they don't even know about yet? What does this suggest about the PINS you should target?

Consider these issues and questions from your own vantage point, and be sure to ask your clients, customers, and prospects for their views too. "I'd like to deepen my relationship with your company," you might say. "How could I provide even more value to you in the future? What events or circumstances are causing your needs to evolve in these ways?" Then, use their answers to determine what target PINS match your business expansion goals.

Are there new ways in which you can deliver your products or services? What new methods of distribution can you create that will draw significant future customer and client response? Changes in distribution can have more lasting impact than changes in the product itself. We need only observe the growth of the huge booksellers on the Internet, led into the fray by amazon.com, to see that a product may remain essentially the same while a company can revolutionize how the product is delivered to the consumer.

What will you want from your business in five years? Fifteen years? What shifts and changes in your business will ensure that it satisfies your vision and your values as you change and grow? What does all this suggest about the PINS you should target?

Keep a finger on the pulse of what's happening in your current and target PINS.

Avid reading and focused attention are essential. On page 30, we offered suggestions for developing good readiness habits as part of a strategy for lifelong learning. These were ways in which to begin enhancing your alliance-ability, preparing yourself and your business for SmartMatch Alliances.

Following are a few beyond-the-basics strategies for staying hyper-aware of what's going on in your current and target PINS . . .

Read, watch, and listen to:

- *Daily and weekly newspapers.* Look for coverage of mergers, acquisitions, new products and services, and new alliance ideas you can adopt or adapt for your business.

- *Newspapers, magazines, and newsletters that serve your current and target PINS.* Look for news of recently promoted people and open job positions. Note these publications' editorial direction, key themes and messages, contributing writers, new and existing alliances. Be a sleuth! Surf the websites of the largest advertisers in these publications, looking for industry trends, specific website links, their alliances—past and present, and other characteristics and activities that might offer valuable insights into their "alliance-ability."

- *Radio and television.* Look and listen for the advertising approaches and methods of big-time advertisers and watch to see how global companies are building their alliances. Think about the ways in which they structure their alliances (something they tend to do very well) and consider how you might be able to adapt their methods and strategies to suit your alliance goals.

- *E-newsletters that serve your PINS.* Look for topic threads and product and service offerings. Click on the website links included in the articles and note what companies' products and services are featured.

Participate in:

- *Professional organizations and associations serving your current and target PINS.* Contribute timely articles to showcase your expertise in their publications and websites, and develop relationships with the centers of influence within these organizations. Look for and get involved with high-visibility and influential committees such as . . .
  - ◆ Membership
  - ◆ New Member Orientation
  - ◆ Program-Planning
  - ◆ Trade Show-Planning
  - ◆ Economic Development (particularly for chambers of commerce)

  Find out as much as possible about these committees (who is on them, what their mission is, how often they meet . . .). Maximize the value of the time you invest in these committees by attending several meetings before selecting those you'd like to join. The committee(s) you join should include the greatest visibility to potential alliance partners.

- *Conferences, trade shows, and conventions where your PINS convene.* Seek out opportunities to speak, exhibit, network, and conduct market research by visiting the booths and other displays of industry exhibitors.

- *In-person networking groups serving your current and target PINS.* Remember that your time is valuable, so be certain to select groups whose members will help you move forward. Cast a critical eye on the methods and standards members follow for exchanging leads and referrals, and the quality of the connections.

- *E-mail discussion groups featuring topics likely to be of interest to your current and target PINS.* Look for who is participating, the volume of messages, the quality of the interchange, and the relevance to your current or future alliance efforts.

Keep track of emerging, significant trends that drive our society and determine the future of many businesses—including perhaps yours! Some examples:

- The Internet has become the distribution channel of choice for businesses from florists to exotic wine merchants to logo design services. What new opportunities will this create for you in your current and target PINS?

- Continued increases in telecommuting create the demand for new home office design services as well as benefits for the companies, benefits for workers, and benefits for the environment. What will the benefits be for your company and how will you serve this growing market with your Smart-Match Alliances?

- In our "post-dot.com" era, we have replaced unbridled enthusiasm for any and all new ideas with a determination to make decisions based on a company's strong foundations and solid underpinnings. How can you fine-tune your filtering systems to ask the questions that will uncover potential alliance partners' integrity and professional business practices?

- Business is no longer constrained by the requirements of geography, e.g., a local chamber of commerce is not the only choice for connecting with prospective customers and clients. If you were to structure a SmartMatch Alliance that expands your reach to a broader regional market—or a national or global one—what new clients and customers could you attract?

- The paradigm of a career-long association with a single employer in which loyalty serves as the cornerstone of the relationship is a thing of the past! In its place is your personal branding, which means that in your career planning efforts, you need to pay continued and careful attention to daily and lifelong learning, staying technology-savvy and current, relying on Internet career resources, and continuously honing your remote and virtual business skills. Do you have a plan for your next career leap—or are you just looking for your next job?

Take a few minutes now to answer these questions in your *Alliance Journal.*

Let Others Do Your Selling

One small company grows in leaps and bounds by letting an alliance partner do the selling.

Who's Who: Our Coaching Success client, David owns a travel services company that specializes in making travel plans for international executives. His alliance partner is a company that provides world-class security services to Fortune 500 companies with a large international presence.

The Goals: David was seeking a way to expand his client base. His alliance partner was seeking to add a second product to its portfolio of customer offerings.

The Exchange: A revenue-sharing SmartMatch Alliance was created, with David providing his web-based training and his alliance partner's international sales team offering the product to their existing large corporation client base.

The Win-Win: Lots and lots of sales to clients that would have taken David's company years and years to develop. In exchange, his alliance partner increased their revenue stream.

The Takeaway: When choosing a SmartMatch Alliance partner, select the very best within your industry and niche. And don't be afraid to let others do your selling!

Get noticed in your PINS.

Make it easy for potential alliance partners in your current and target PINS to find you, impress them with your professionalism and expertise, and increase your appeal as a potential alliance partner. Each of the following strategies will help you gain visibility and exposure in your PINS. (As a bonus, the increased exposure you'll get will help you sell more products and services along the way!)

Write articles that showcase your expertise. Submit them to publications and organizations serving your PINS.

Articles on topics of interest to the people and businesses in your current and target PINS help to position you and your company as expert and influential. Even more important for the purposes of SmartMatch Alliances, these articles and the resulting exposure make you a much more attractive alliance partner!

A good length for an article is 700 to 1,000 words, since this is the size most frequently published. If you have good writing skills, with a little organization and practice, a new article will take you only an hour or two to complete.

If, on the other hand, you're concerned about your writing skills, consider hiring a professional writer, one who communicates well with business and professional people and can translate your ideas and approach. If you can find a writer who actually lives in your world and understands your PINS, all the better!

Here are some ideas for articles you might write to showcase your expertise to the people and businesses in your current and target PINS:

- new research impacting your PINS
- new or pending legislation influencing your PINS
- trends, discoveries, and developments affecting your PINS
- Internet trends involving your PINS
- survey results of interest to your PINS
- "how-to" articles that demonstrate your knowledge and expertise to your PINS

Articles on topics like these will enable you to position yourself to become "top of mind" for prospective alliance partners, increasing the likelihood that they will contact you.

The key to writing great articles is providing interesting information that's timely and germane to the professionals and businesses in your PINS. Good articles showcase your expertise and offer something of value to your readers . . . with NO sales promotion. Remember: articles are not brochures. They're not flyers or newsletters about your business. They are a meaty, weighty, quick, good read of information readers can use or will find interesting.

High Demand

The great news is that the demand is high for well-written articles that offer real information and value. Industry and professional organizations in particular are always looking for articles that speak to their members. Satisfy this demand regularly with quality articles, and you will intensify your exposure, enhance your reputation, and increase your irresistibility as a potential alliance partner with your current and target PINS.

Search the library for associations that serve your PINS. Get acquainted with the reference librarian, who is often a great resource with a broad base of knowledge on just about everything!

Buy or consult *The Association YELLOWBOOK* (published by *Leadership Directories,* www.leadershipdirectories.com) to find 1,100-plus listings of leading U.S. trade and professional organizations. You might also talk directly to people in your current and target PINS and ask what associations and industry groups they belong to.

The Internet is also a powerful tool in your quest to identify organizations and communities where the greatest numbers of your potential alliance partners congregate. (This is, in fact, one of the most valuable applications of this powerful technology: specifically, using the Internet to find communities, locate people and businesses in your PINS, and bring people together from all over the world.)

Once you identify these organizations, search their websites or call to find out about the publications they produce for their members. We guarantee there will be at least one magazine or E-newsletter for each trade or professional organization.

Trade publications that serve your current and target PINS are another outlet for your articles. If you wanted to create a SmartMatch Alliance that enabled you to sell more equipment to hog farmers, for instance, you might write articles on the latest technologies powering hog-farming equipment or proven techniques for keeping your hog-farming equipment in good working order and send them in to *Hog Farmer* magazine. If your articles are published, one of the publication's major advertisers—perhaps a leading fertilizer company—might see them and then later on be more receptive to speaking with you about the possibility of building a SmartMatch Alliance as a result.

Focus In

Narrow your list of associations and publications down to those that serve the greatest number of individuals and businesses in your PINS. Decide whether having your articles read by the members of a given association or the target audiences of a given publication will further your goal of increased visibility within your PINS with the ultimate aim of being more appealing to high-potential alliance partners. Ask yourself:

- "If my articles appear in this association newsletter or trade publication, will they be read by great numbers of individuals and businesses in my current and target PINS?"

- "Will having my articles appear in this association newsletter or trade publication make me visible to potential alliance partners and/or increase my exposure so that I am more attractive to potential alliance partners?"

- "Will having my articles appear in this association newsletter or trade publication enable me to increase my number of E-newsletter subscribers, which will then increase my EOV options, thereby making me more attractive to a potential alliance partner?"

- "Will having my articles appear in this association newsletter or trade publication enhance my image and/or my company's image when included in my media clippings and publication credits?"

- "Will having my articles appear in this association newsletter or trade publication lead to interest on the part of other publications serving my current and/or target PINS?"

The Scoop on Writer's Guidelines

Here is an excerpt of the article submission guidelines for a national magazine:

Manuscripts must be double-spaced with at least a two-inch right-hand margin. Please place the following information in the footer on each page:

- *Article title*
- *Date*
- *Draft number*
- *Your name*
- *Contact information (phone, fax, E-mail address)*

Manuscripts must be submitted electronically (no faxes, please), either on disk or as an E-mail attachment. In either case, file format must be Word for Windows 6.0 or lower.

- "Will having my articles appear in this association newsletter or trade publication lead to media interviews that will be heard by individuals and businesses in my current and/or target PINS?"

Make Contact

Once you've narrowed down your list to the association newsletters and trade publications that will be read by large numbers of individuals and businesses in your current and target PINS, contact the person who leads the editorial staff of each of the organizations and publications you've selected. Within an organization, this will be the president or executive director. Within a publication, this person may have a title like business editor, managing editor, or simply editor.

Explain that you're interested in submitting an article for publication and request article-submission guidelines (or writer's guidelines). These guidelines provide information about each publication's target audience, frequency, and editorial platform or mission . . . information you need to help you determine the likelihood that your articles will be read by the prospective alliance partners you're targeting.

Writer's guidelines vary from one organization or publication to another, ranging from the very formal and precise to the more informal and nonspecific (to the nonexistent!), but it's essential to respect and adhere to these guidelines no matter what. They may include some or all of the following:

- the overall theme of the issue of the publication to which you're contributing
- the general subject and specific topic to be covered, including any special notes or concerns
- the specific positioning of the article based on the industry's, profession's, and/or organization's view, business objectives, or position on current events
- specific requests for material to be treated in sidebars
- article length, usually expressed as a word count

- deadline for a first draft
- turnaround time on any changes the editor may request

Ask for the publication's editorial calendar, a document that shows the theme of each upcoming issue. This information will enable you to tailor your articles to the subject matter of a given issue, allowing you to provide greater value and content that's a better fit. For example, the March issue of *Accounting Education News* will focus on "solid practice principles." What might you write about if you'd like to attract a CPA alliance partner?

Pitch Your Idea

After reviewing the writer's guidelines and editorial calendar, send an enticing (and friendly!) cover letter (sometimes called a "pitch" letter) to the person who heads up the editorial staff at each association and/or publication. This pitch letter can be sent through the postal service, by fax, or via E-mail depending on the guidelines of the specific publication.

Regardless of how you send it, use the letter to summarize the content of your article and highlight your expertise. Consider including statements like:

- "I live in the world of your readers, members, and/or subscribers; I have extensive expertise in this niche or specialty."
- "I regularly work with your readers, members, and/or subscribers clients, customers, prospects, members, subscribers, and/or website visitors."
- "My articles are information-rich and written to help readers become more effective . . . never commercials for my company, products, or services! Each one is filled with tips, trends, and techniques written specifically for your readers."

- "I am technology-savvy and can submit my article in any form you require."
- "This is just one of many such articles. In fact, I write a free article each month. Would you like to see a list of pertinent articles that are available for reprint?"

Other Channels

Once your articles are developed, bear in mind that they are your intellectual capital (your ideas and insights that are intangible but highly valuable assets), which you can (and will!) use and reuse in a variety of valuable ways.

In addition to being made accessible to associations and publications that serve the professionals and businesses in your current and target PINS, completed articles can be:

- sent directly to potential alliance partners by E-mail, fax, or mail (Of course you will also send them to your clients and prospects as a value-added part of your relationship!)
- placed on specific industry and professional websites—a powerful alliance magnet
- sent to your potential alliance partners' industry and professional publications
- used as a foundation for training (For instance, a "how to" piece or series can be used to educate alliance partners about your work, experience, resources, and expertise.)
- placed in a workbook and given to audience members when you're making a speech. (Carefully selected speaking engagements are another powerful magnet for alliance partners . . . keep reading!)
- included in a package of materials you provide when meeting with an alliance partner for the first time. (These articles will help to enhance your image and credibility with the potential alliance partner.)

You might also choose to post past articles on your website. Again, these are your intellectual property to do with as you wish. Some of our clients choose to archive their articles, which means they include all back articles on their website and permit visitors, including potential alliance partners, to click on a topic of interest and read the piece online.

We, and others like us, prefer to list past articles and permit visitors to request back issues, instead of providing unlimited, uncontrolled access to our intellectual property. This approach:

- alerts us to the articles and topics that are most in demand (a bit of free and easy market research for us)
- enables us to gain E-newsletter subscribers from interested readers and visitors to our website

You might want to have your articles mentioned within an industry website, E-mail discussion group, or E-newsletter. Here are some specific tips for doing so in ways that add to your alliance-ability:

- Use a search engine to find specific E-mail discussion groups for your PINS. Join the group, observe the customs and topics, and begin submitting responses relevant to the topics at hand. Include your contact information and a descriptive phrase in your E-Mail signature, the standard text that you set to automatically appear at the end of each E-mail you send.
- Use your search engine to find pertinent websites that accept article submissions.

Regardless of the communication channel through which you decide to send your articles to gain intense exposure to potential alliance partners in your PINS, be certain to aim the content of your articles to people at a decision-maker level. Picture yourself sitting across the table from a decision maker, perhaps over lunch. What would you say? What advice would you want to impart that could improve this person's business or career from the vantage point of your expertise? This strategy enables you to become visible and valuable to the people with the power and authority to take the next step in the process of building a SmartMatch Alliance with you.

Paid or Free?

Over the years, some of our coaching clients have wondered whether they ought to ask the editor or publisher of a given publication for a fee for their articles. We advise them to offer their articles for free—as a general rule. Doing so accomplishes two things. First, it increases the number of people who will read the articles (there's a much bigger market for free articles than for paid ones), and, since the goal is exposure, that's beneficial.

Second, if a publication pays for the articles, there's a good chance it's buying some rights to the material . . . first-publication rights, reprint rights, and the like. This may restrict your ability to use and re-use your intellectual property in unlimited ways. Giving up this autonomy generally isn't worth the small amount a given publication may be willing to pay you for your article.

Instead of remuneration for your article, require that your contact information and "bio box" be included at the top or bottom of your articles. This means always send your contact information with your articles, including your E-mail address, full name, company name, website address, phone, and fax. Whatever subset of this information they decide to include will serve you well. For example, *Fast Company* magazine often includes only E-mail addresses for its contributing writers—but that's worth a lot!

Your advantage is obvious, but the publication also wins because it's providing a way for its members or subscribers and other readers to contact you for more helpful information on the important topic at hand.

Expertise, Commitment . . . and Exposure!

When you share your industry knowledge, unique insights into professional developments in your PINS, reactions to trends, and tips your potential alliance partners can use, these readers will be impressed by your expertise and commitment to their industry or profession. For potential alliance partners within your target PINS, this will mean you have positioned yourself as an visible, accessible, and acknowledged expert— which will attract perfect alliance partners faster.

When your articles are placed with this kind of professional and industry visibility, the reader (that is, your potential alliance partners) will read what you have to share on two levels. On the first level, they'll read your articles, be impressed with your knowledge, and may contact you and your company to learn more about your products and services.

On a second and deeper level, the people reading your articles will realize that you and your company are experts within your field, which is why your articles were selected over those of other authors and companies.

Here's the magic of this strategy: a potential alliance partner reads your article in this month's industry or profession magazine, loves it, realizes your brilliance, and immediately visits your website. They instantly see that you and your company live in their world and understand the concerns, issues, and problems they face. They know you have the values and insights that will get them out of a fix or deliver them to the next business breakthrough in their industry or profession. They contact your company and become a client or subscribe to your free E-newsletter.

Now, as they watch you work, read your articles, reply to your surveys, attend your TeleForums, etc. (see page 63 for a concise definition and strategies for hosting TeleForums), they decide to contact you to explore the possibility of a working relationship. This, of course, will open the door for you to dis-

SmartNote

Because of the way in which SmartMatch Alliances are structured, disappointments are rare, but some disappointment is a natural consequence of trying anything new.

Make a policy of learning from your alliance mistakes and disappointments rather than being discouraged by them. Ask yourself, "What did I do right in this alliance?" and "What will I do differently next time?"

Record your answers in your *Alliance Journal.* Check these learning experiences and make immediate adjustments so they don't turn into ongoing problems. As we like to tell our coaching clients, learning from mistakes is a two-step process: you've got to drain the swamp AND remove the alligators!

cuss a possible SmartMatch Alliance. We see it happening all the time, in our business and in our clients' businesses!

Create an E-newsletter

An E-newsletter is a terrific way to stay in touch with the individuals and businesses in your current and target PINS with frequency and regularity. Your E-newsletter might include your free monthly articles—plus some newsworthy information of value and interest to subscribers (e.g., announcements of upcoming seminars or TeleForums). Because it is created from your own writing, an E-newsletter dovetails nicely with the exposure strategy of writing articles and submitting them to the association newsletters and trade publications that serve your PINS.

An E-newsletter may take a number of forms, but its main purpose is to communicate with a growing community of subscribers (think potential alliance partners) and offer them timely and impactful content. The more subscribers you have, the larger your base of potential alliance partners since a number of your subscribers are likely to become alliance partners. Bear in mind that 1,500 subscribers is a reasonable initial goal for a small business, but consider the possibilities you'll have with 50,000 or 500,000 E-newsletter subscribers—whether yours is a small, medium, or large business.

A growing subscriber base gives you exponential leverage by rapidly increasing the number of times your E-newsletter is forwarded to others (complete with your subscription and contact information, of course!). This will deliver even more potential alliance partners to you. And an E-newsletter with a substantial number of subscribers makes you more appealing as a potential SmartMatch Alliance partner because it is a powerful marketing and visibility asset for an EOV (you'll find more on EOVs starting on page 80).

To produce an E-newsletter, you must first determine its primary and any secondary audiences, overall length, and distribution frequency. Your best choice for frequency might be monthly or weekly, since a daily E-newsletter will require a greater investment of time and other resources. Remember, the goal is to be visible and stay in touch with your PINS on a regular basis, not to inundate your subscribers with time-wasting E-mails.

Next, decide the type of content you'd like to include in your E-newsletter: feature articles that tackle a current issue or trend, insights and opinion pieces, industry surveys, tools and techniques for problem solving, industry or legislative news. You might also have regular features such as a "60-Second Sales Clinic" or a "Customer Service Corner."

If you don't want to write all the content for the E-newsletter yourself, you might consider using other writers (with permission from the author and appropriate attribution in your E-newsletter).

Note that to truly capitalize on the repetition value of your E-newsletter as a alliance-attraction engine, some consistency in its content—regular features, a consistent layout, a uniform tone of voice, and the like—is helpful. Your readers will like this predictability, and it will help them to identify your E-newsletter with you and your company . . . and help you break through the clutter of news and information they're exposed to each day.

Consider the tone of the writing that will appeal to your E-newsletter's target audiences . . . is it relaxed and conversational or perhaps more buttoned-up and pinstriped? Something in between? This is essential for making certain that your E-newsletter speaks directly to the individuals and businesses in your current and target PINS. It makes your content inviting and helps to build a community that clients and subscribers feel they belong to.

Creating and Building a List of Subscribers

The topic of how to create an E-mail list of subscribers who would like to receive your E-newsletter could fill three volumes by itself. Here are some general—but essential—guidelines:

- Begin to build your E-newsletter list with the names of everyone you know—including your clients, customers, and, of course, potential alliance partners.

- Encourage subscribers to forward a copy of your newsletter to colleagues they believe would be interested in its content.

- Make it as easy as possible for people to subscribe. Include a subscription opportunity in every E-mail you send, at the end of each issue of your E-newsletter, and in a prominent place on your website. Be certain it's clear that there is no charge to subscribe. (The word "free" is very enticing!)

- Provide subscription information in every author's note or bio box you include with the articles you submit to the association newsletters and trade publications read by the individuals and businesses in your PINS.

- Offer a hard copy of your free E-newsletter at meetings, gatherings of networking groups, and at your speeches and presentations. (Include subscription information in the hard copy, of course!)

- Mention your E-newsletter during media interviews.

- Include subscription information in your E-mail "signature file" or tag line.

- Include a mention of your E-newsletter and website address on your business cards.

- Form strategic alliances with other organizations that have large numbers of E-newsletter subscribers.

And please remember, one of the best ways to build your subscriber base is to write excellent, meaty articles that offer readers and potential alliance partners quality information they're inspired to forward to their clients and colleagues. Nothing is more appealing than genuinely good work.

Bear in mind too that each activity which increases the size of your subscriber list and/or number of your website visitors enhances—often dramatically—your ability to attract SmartMatch Alliance partners.

Become a Board Member within the professional organizations and associations serving your PINS

We've already encouraged you to join these organizations and associations (review page 46). Consider the added exposure and leverage afforded by participation in the organization's board of directors. Board participation enables you to rub elbows with an industry's or profession's major players, offering you the opportunity to watch trends, improve your ability to anticipate—and capitalize on!—shifts that might impact potential alliances and/or current alliance partners. Examples include innovations or recent discoveries, emerging trends, new technologies, pending and recently enacted legislation, and new competitive threats and opportunities.

Host Free TeleForums

Technology has made it quick, easy, and cost-effective to host teleconference calls for three or three hundred participants from around the country or around the world.

You can access this technology and invite your clients, prospects, and even potential alliance partners to join a free teleconference call led by you and others in your company. These calls have the power to rapidly increase your exposure and the awareness of your superior product offerings and/or expertise in your current and target PINS.

TeleForums, our signature approach to using teleconference technology as a distance-learning tool, are easy and cost-effective . . . and they're quickly becoming the meeting and training venue of choice for leading companies around the world. We've also found that TeleForums are an ideal alliance vehicle.

Here are two ways we use TeleForums and help our clients use them:

1. Free TeleForums: These are a powerful attraction vehicle that helps you gain subscribers, build trust, and plant seeds for the future. They also enable participants to become familiar with the products and services you and your company sell. Increased trust and familiarity make for increased revenue.

2. Paid TeleForums: These can provide an exciting revenue stream for you and your business. TeleForum participants pay from $29 to $129 for a 60-minute call, and enjoy convenient, cost-effective learning experiences. In the aggregate, these fees provide substantial revenues for a given business or for alliance partners within a SmartMatch Alliance. Combining TeleForums with the right SmartMatch

What Is a TeleForum™?

Our coaching services are delivered by telephone in a format we call a TeleForum. A TeleForum uses a workshop format in a 60-minute interactive telephone conference call. Coaching Success TeleForums work with a cohesive group of clients in a given company, profession, niche, industry, or association.

During a typical TeleForum, participants receive insight, information, feedback, coaching, resources, tips, tools, techniques, and valuable new ideas.

Each TeleForum is easily accessed by telephone, which means participants join the meeting, participate, and experience a lively and informative exchange of ideas from the convenience of their own offices or homes . . . with no travel expense!

Alliance partner can bring $1 million or more per year in sales and profits to the alliance.

Our TeleForum model stresses ease, convenience, and cost-effectiveness. We've spent many years perfecting this model and making it available to our coaching clients and SmartMatch Alliance partners. No special technology is necessary to adopt the TeleForum model, and, where teleconference calls using the phone company's technology can run into many hundreds or thousands of dollars for a one-hour call, our TeleForum model uses special technology that enables you and your company to host a TeleForum at a small fraction of the phone company costs.

Within a SmartMatch Alliance, you might use a TeleForum to:

- showcase your alliance partner
- introduce your alliance partner as a sponsor of the TeleForum
- deliver a joint presentation with your alliance partner featuring—
  - the information offered in your most recent article
  - the findings of an industry-specific focus group
  - pressing legal issues
  - new marketing ideas
  - Internet trends impacting an industry and/or profession
  - techniques for increasing revenues and profits
  - sales training
  - technical training
  - announcements of new products or organizational changes
  - well-known industry authors and speakers presenting on their area of expertise

To begin including TeleForums in your "alliance-generating" strategy, you would:

1. Schedule the date and time of the TeleForum.
2. Choose your topics.
3. Select and set up the TeleForum conference call technology.
4. Determine the cost (if any) to participants, and handle the payments.
5. Invite your customers, clients, subscribers, prospects, vendors, and potential alliance partners.
6. Send an E-mail invitation that includes registration instructions.
7. Handle registrations and send each participant a confirmation.
8. Send a reminder E-mail notice to registered participants in advance of the TeleForum.
9. Facilitate and coach the participants during the TeleForum.
10. Send a post-TeleForum follow-up that invites additional feedback and includes your contact information.

One important caveat: before you attempt to run your first TeleForums, *get some coaching*. TeleForums are highly interactive and must honor the best principles in adult learning. When you honor these principles, you and the participants receive the benefits of shared wisdom, increased retention of information, and optimal results. Familiarize yourself and your presenters—internal and external—with these principles before attempting to conduct a TeleForum yourself.

Specifically, you'll need coaching on how to:

- structure an engaging, valuable TeleForum
- prepare for the TeleForum (including guidance on how to schedule the TeleForum, use the technology, send invitations, and handle registrations, confirmations, and reminders, etc.)

- determine the internal and external experts who will participate in each TeleForum: by title, by responsibility, by geography, by time zone, by need, by area of expertise
- determine the outline and information to cover and what material, if any, needs to be sent in advance
- "frame" each TeleForum: "What is the purpose of each call?"
- facilitate and coach a variety of personalities and behavior styles
- know you're having a positive impact during the TeleForum
- use laughter and humor effectively and appropriately
- stay focused throughout the TeleForum, especially when the discussion might be moving in an unintended direction
- pay attention to the pace and tempo of the TeleForum

For our TeleForums we communicate exclusively by E-mail. Based on our research and experience, E-mail is the most efficient and cost-effective way to communicate to a large audience of E-newsletter subscribers, participants, and potential alliance partners. The subscriber list we use for our alliance announcements is the very same list we've judiciously and respectfully compiled and used in all our business-development efforts, including the distribution of our free monthly E-newsletter aimed at increasing our exposure and marketing visibility in our current and target PINS.

Our TeleForum invitations include each of the following elements:

1. *Who* will get the most from the TeleForum?
2. *What* topic or subject will be covered?
3. *When* will it be held?

4. *Why* would participants want to attend? What benefits will they gain?

5. *How* will participants receive the phone number to call in and participate in the TeleForum?

Here's an example of a TeleForum invitation we used for the AllianceWizard TeleForums we held when SMARTMATCH ALLIANCES was being written:

We are pleased to be sharing with you the news of our new book (to be published in September) plus a new TeleForum series!

Each month we will bring you a new/free Coaching Success AllianceWizard TeleForum™, based on our book called "SmartMatch Alliances," which will be published in September. Our next TeleForum will be on Tuesday, January 8th at 11:30 a.m. New York time. To register for this TeleForum or to learn more about our book, please visit our AllianceWizard page at www.coachingsuccess.com/alliancewizard.html.

Have a sunshine day!

The Coaches, Judy and Ernest

. . . .

COACHING SUCCESS TELEFORUMS™: January Schedule

. . . .

Free *AllianceWizard* TeleForum™

Our next AllianceWizard TeleForum™ will be on Tuesday, January 8th at 11:30 a.m. New York time. Our topic for this AllianceWizard TeleForum™ will be "Your Strategic Alliance... Get It Right The First Time" and we will discuss...

==> What kind of up-front alliance design is necessary/required?

==> Alliance pitfalls...and how to avoid them!

==> Tips for maintaining and growing your SmartMatch Alliance!

. . . .

If you would like to participate in our AllianceWizard TeleForum™:

1. Please reserve your calendar for the correct date, Tuesday, January 8th.

2. Please note, the above TeleForum starts at 11:30 a.m. EST/New York time, which is

10:30 a.m./CST/Dallas time

9:30 a.m./MST/Denver time

8:30 a.m./PST/San Francisco time

3. You can register for this free session and receive the telephone number to call by going to our AllianceWizard page at www.coachingsuccess.com/alliancewizard.html or by sending an E-mail to register@coachingsuccess.com with "AllianceWizard TeleForum" in the subject line. In the body please put your:

Company Name:

Your Name:

E-mail Address:

Telephone Number:

City/State/Country:

Profession or Position:

Website:

• •

For an E-mail subscription send a message to subscribe@coachingsuccess.com or subscribe at our website: www.coachingsuccess.com

• •

To remove yourself from this list, send an E-mail to the same address, replacing "subscribe" with "unsubscribe."

• •

We will NEVER release, sell or give a subscriber's name or E-mail address to any other party or organization. Our subscribers will only receive E-mail messages that contain requested information, new monthly articles, or announcements of new services.

• •

Judy and Ernest are master business coaches with international coaching practices that include a wide variety of executives, business owners and professional people. They work with their clients by telephone and E-mail, specializing in global distance learning by telephone, using their state-of-the-art conference call system for interactive and dynamic TeleForums. TeleForums link 10-100 executives/professionals/individuals who are geographically dispersed, in a time-efficient and profitable format. Recent articles have appeared 3,000-plus times in business/trade publications and websites.

• •

As always, it's great to be in touch with our subscribers in 70-plus countries...{Argentina, Australia, Austria, Barbados, Bahrain, Belgium, Bolivia, Brazil, Bulgaria, Canada, Czech Republic, China, Colombia, Costa Rica, Croatia, Cuba, Denmark, Egypt, Ethiopia, Finland, France, Germany, Guam, Guatemala, Honduras, Hungary, Ireland, India, Indonesia, Israel, Italy, Japan, Kenya, Korea, Malaysia, Mexico, Namibia, Netherlands, New Zealand, Nicaragua, Nigeria, Norway, Pakistan, Peru, Philippines, Poland, Portugal, Romania, Russia, Saudi Arabia, Scotland, Singapore, South Africa, Spain, Sweden, Switzerland, Syria, Ukraine, United Arab Emirates, United Kingdom, USA, Thailand, Turkey, Trinidad, Venezuela, Vietnam, The Virgin Islands, Yemen, Yugoslavia, and Zimbabwe}.

• •

Delight your friends and colleagues by suggesting they subscribe to our FREE Coaching Success Newsletter! Subscription requests should be E-mailed to subscribe@coachingsuccess.com

Speak at industry, professional, and educational events

These include trade shows, conventions, and sales and executive meetings. These highly visible and well-attended events enable you to further establish your expertise and product or service offerings to people and businesses in your current and target PINS.

Begin by sharpening your mental picture of the perfect audience for your information and expertise. Who are they? Where do they convene in groups? What are their interests, professional hot buttons, and goals? (If you're stumped, try envisioning the characteristics of the audiences you want to avoid. This process of elimination can be a great way to identify your ideal audience!) Take out your *Alliance Journal* and record your answers. Consider asking people within your PINS for their ideas.

Finding Opportunities

Industry and professional organizations often find speakers by reading industry, professional, and trade publications, seeing articles they like and noting the name and expertise of the author. They may then invite this person to be an expert speaker at their next luncheon or dinner meeting. This is another reason to write articles designed to appeal to the interests and information needs of the people and businesses you most want to reach . . . and to the alliance partners with the highest potential!

Find other speaking opportunities by checking the business section of your daily newspaper and local business publications for meeting announcements. Look for business and professional organizations, chambers of commerce, women's groups, civic organizations, universities, and schools. Contact the organizers of the meetings that are likely to attract the people in your current and target PINS. Describe your background and message, and ask whether they use speakers and presenters at their meetings. Provide a list of topics you can speak on at future meetings. If you can't get on their calendar in the short term, schedule a date when you can and offer to be an alternate speaker who can fill in if someone cancels.

Concentrate on finding groups and audiences already assembled for you, for instance, trade, industry, and professional organizations, community groups, and the like. Aim for groups of at least 30 to 50 people. For larger groups, connect with convention centers, meeting planners, and speakers' bureaus.

Paid or Free?

Our coaching clients sometimes wonder whether it's wise to charge these organizations for delivering their presentations.

If speaking and training are a significant revenue source for you, ask to be paid top dollar.

If speaking and training are not a significant revenue source for you, consider these four factors:

1. the projected size of the audience (i.e. the potential level of exposure)
2. the composition of the group (how likely the group is to contain high-potential prospects and alliance partners)
3. the likelihood of turning a potential alliance partner into an active alliance partner
4. the time required to prepare your presentation

Take into account each of these factors when you're deciding whether to accept an invitation to speak before a group. Then:

- Ask for a reduced or "lite" fee when some of the four factors above are in your favor and align well with your alliance-building goals.
- Speak for free when all four factors are in your favor and align well with your alliance-building goals. The exposure will be well worth it!

In the traditional meeting model, you will be invited to speak in person on a particular day and time for this upcoming event. Recently, however, the concept of virtual presentations has gained momentum. Imagine being paid $5,000 for two hours of your time to make a presentation to your perfect audience anywhere in the world—without leaving your office. In these virtual presentations, the audience is assembled in one location, and the presenter speaks from another (remote) location by phone, by video plus phone (i.e., videoconferencing), or via the Internet. The audience's view of the speaker ranges from a static photo projected on a screen to real-time video. Now that's powerful exposure and visibility!

Use Your Website Effectively

One of the strategies for getting noticed by a potential alliance partner is to drive traffic to your website. Therefore, it's essential that you use your website effectively.

Take a few moments to visit your website and answer these questions as objectively as possible:

1. As a whole, does your website (design, message, size, links) reflect the experience, image, integrity, etc. of you and your company?
2. Does your home page instantly speak what we call the "language of value" to potential alliance partners? Does it clearly state what you do, how well you do it, and the depth of your commitment to performance and service?
3. Can visitors easily find articles that speak to their needs? Will they capture the attention of a potential alliance partner?
4. Does your website mention your involvement with the PINS you serve?
5. Can visitors register for an upcoming free Tele-Forum or subscribe to your E-newsletter?
6. Can visitors find a schedule of your in-person and virtual presentations?
7. Does your website engage your visitors by requiring them to take an action step to extract the information they need?

Use these seven areas as a checklist for possible improvement. Tackle one at a time in the order that is easiest and most
natural for you and your company. A small upgrade in your
website can produce a large improvement in your alliance-
ability! The main idea is continuous improvement. The

Vroom!

How can you be certain you've taken the right steps to
make yourself and your business visible and appealing to
potential SmartMatch Alliance partners? Think *VROOM!*

- **Visibility.** You are easy to find and communicate with.

- **Reputation.** You have unique positioning, a sterling
  brand name, and a solid reputation for excellence
  and superior performance.

- **Offer.** A good offer that an alliance partner would be
  willing to share with their prospects, clients, and customers. Be certain your products and services are up
  to snuff, reasonably priced, and a great value for the
  client or customer.

- **Outlook.** A positive outlook and mindset about
  alliances as a high-potential strategy for business
  expansion.

- **Message.** A solid message that reflects unique positioning and that is repeated with consistency. Your key
  messages appear consistently in your promotional
  material and appropriately reflect you and your company, your expertise, and your products and services.

Internet is a dynamic medium. Change your approach, your content, your visitors' experience . . . often and with excellence!

Know your competition.

Every successful business owner or savvy executive has a firm handle 'on the competition—the professionals and businesses competing for market share within their PINS. They know the products and services their competitors offer, their prices, their positioning, and their strategic alliances.

Strengthen your competitive intelligence within your current and target PINS. Sharply focus your attention on the strategic alliances being created by your competitors. Look for how these alliances were created, what's being offered through the alliance, how the alliance is being marketed, and perhaps clues to the financial arrangement.

Be aware of competitive information by regularly reviewing:

- *Computer databases and websites such as monster.com and Dun & Bradstreet.* (These will tell you who's hiring, who's expanding, and who's initiating new projects or programs.)

- *Directories such as membership and manufacturers' directories.* (You'll find out about who's in, who's out, and what websites to research. These directories also measure the size, scope, and power of these organizations.)

- *Technical specifications and any literature shipped with a competitor's product you might have ordered.* (This material tells you a lot about your competitors' customer service and level of technological sophistication.)

- *Competitors' promotional materials and advertisements.* (These are a window into your competitors' "best foot forward" and latest products and services.)

AIDA (. . . *and you thought it was just an opera!*)

Getting potential alliance partners to notice you is a process that takes time. In traditional advertising circles, this process is referred to as a chain of events and dubbed AIDA: Awareness, Interest, Desire, and then Action.

Here's our take on this time-honored process from the vantage point of attracting potential SmartMatch Alliance partners—

- **Awareness:** A potential alliance partner hears you speak, reads your article, visits your website, or is referred to you by someone within your current or target PINS. They have become aware of you and your company.

- **Interest:** A potential alliance partner becomes intrigued by one or more of your products, services, or offerings, and wants to learn more about you and your company. At this point in the process, the potential partner may send you an E-mail or make a phone call as an initial contact.

- **Desire:** Your response to their inquiry and your introduction of the idea for a potential alliance has them intrigued, and both parties want to move forward with some alliance conversations.

- **Action:** As a result of this preliminary contact, you exchange a few alliance E-mails, schedule a few phone calls, and proceed to craft a SmartMatch Alliance.

Living Deep Within Your Niche . . . The Dream Alliance

Here's a firsthand example of the benefits of living deep within your niche.

Who's Who: Tim, a Coaching Success client, is executive director of a regional publishing and advertising sales association. The association's membership is comprised of publishing entrepreneurs who are always reaching for new heights of achievement and success. Coaching Success, our own SmartMatch Alliance, was looking to get deeper into this niche and wanted to build a SmartMatch Alliance with this association.

The Goals: Our goal was to gain more visibility within Tim's industry and to increase the number of our coaching clients in the publishing industry. The association's goal was to provide valuable content for their publisher members.

The EOV: We provided free monthly articles on successful advertising sales strategies and important circulation tips for their members. In addition, we made our teleconference system available for the association's board of directors meetings. We also joined these Board meetings and provided professional insights, coaching, and a view of future trends. Ultimately, we also delivered a series of free TeleForums for their publisher members, positioning ourselves as expert presenters on topics of interest to association members.

The Win-Win: The tremendous amount of exposure we received led to lots and lots of new publisher coaching clients. The association increased the satisfaction of its publisher members by providing content that helped members grow professionally and financially.

The Takeaway: Identify the niche in which you want to increase your visibility. Develop an alliance with their association. Be generous in providing value and the clients and revenue will follow.

- *Competitors' annual reports.* (These provide insight into the future direction, challenges, and risks facing these companies.)

- *Trade shows.* (Scan display booths, pick up literature and information, talk to competitors' employees, and listen to their sales presentations.)

- *Suppliers.* (These people can offer information on market trends and offer insights that may help to sharpen your awareness of competitors' activities.)

- *Your daily newspaper.* (A "must-read" if you do business in your local area!)

- *Articles and news releases in business, trade, and professional publications and journals.* (These offer ideas and insights into competitors' activities.)

Finally, if possible, experience competitors' strategic alliances. Sample what's being offered, sold, or presented.

Building exposure within your current PINS requires focus, patience, and creativity. As you garner broader and broader visibility, you'll begin to see how this investment of time and energy provides the greatest return of any investment you and your company might make.

As you build awareness of your knowledge and expertise within your PINS, watch your community expand and see new business opportunities, growing sales and profits, and alliance partners reaching out for you and your organization.

Use these strategies for increasing your visibility within your PINS—use them! They are a powerful, proven means of drawing potential alliance partners to you that will have an exponential impact on your success.

And remember . . . enjoy the journey as well as the results.

We're ready to **Zoom In on High-Potential Partners!**

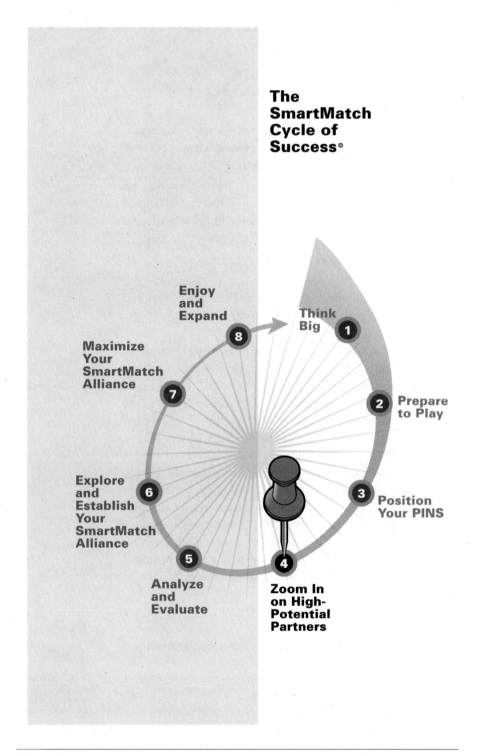

The
SmartMatch
Cycle of
Success©

Think Big **1**

Prepare to Play **2**

Position Your PINS **3**

Zoom In on High-Potential Partners **4**

Analyze and Evaluate **5**

Explore and Establish Your SmartMatch Alliance **6**

Maximize Your SmartMatch Alliance **7**

Enjoy and Expand **8**

Step 4
Zoom In on High-Potential Partners

Your next step is to begin thinking specifically about the alliances and alliance partners you'd like to pursue.

 WHY?

Consider your reasons for pursuing a SmartMatch Alliance (also known as: What's in it for you and your company?).

What results would you like your SmartMatch Alliance to produce? Would your ideal alliance generate more sales? Attract new prospects? Streamline your operations? Expand your Internet presence? Strengthen your own brand or enable you to team up with other powerful brands? How soon would you like all of this to happen?

An Important Note from the Coaches

We strongly encourage you to complete each step of the SmartMatch Alliance process in sequence. Fill out the worksheets, work through each checklist, and make lists in your *Alliance Journal*. Consider building a SmartMatch Alliances file of materials you can refer back to as needed. Learn by doing!

Give these questions some careful thought and record your responses in your *Alliance Journal*. The more specifically you consider these ideal outcomes, the more targeted your alliance-building efforts will be and the more likely they'll be to produce the results you're after.

Here are some outcomes drawn from SmartMatch Alliances we've built for our ourselves, and with our coaching clients:

- generate more profits
- retain more clients
- charge more for products and services
- attract a wider variety of prospects
- encourage buyers to buy low-overhead, but highly profitable services (for example, online banking)
- help make operations seamless, i.e, very easy for the buyer or customer to be served
- significantly increase website traffic
- considerably increase the number of E-newsletter subscribers
- develop multiple streams of passive income
- introduce a new brand created by the alliance
- use one alliance to attract several more alliances
- do all this, and take vacations too!

 WHAT?

List the marketing and visibility assets you can offer to alliance partners.

An alliance is a natural process of give-and-take between partners. We call this give-and-take the SmartMatch Alliance Exchange of Value or EOV.

Potential alliance partners will look carefully at what you bring to the table . . . specifically marketing and visibility assets such as:

Publications

- your E-newsletter with a large subscriber list

- a publication, magazine, or newsletter with a large circulation distributed by hard copy through the postal service
- the ability to write articles for E-newsletters or other publications

TeleForums

- regular TeleForums delivered to individuals and businesses in your current and target PINS

Website

- a comprehensive and powerful website that reflects best practices in your industry or profession
- a website with high visitor volume
- high sales volume through your online store

Visibility

- frequent trade show attendance with high visibility and exposure
- high visibility and a strong reputation within your PINS
- a radio or TV show

Branding

- strong branding and name recognition
- a solid retail presence
- a powerful marketing and advertising engine that consistently strengthens your company's brand name
- a unique service or expertise that an alliance partner's clients would value

Business Model and Track Record

- a strong sales force with high sales volume potential

- a visionary leadership team committed to, and seriously interested in, alliances
- a consistent track record of success and profitability

Use the checklist on the following page to list your marketing/visibility tools. Take enough time to finish this process so your final list reflects every marketing and visibility asset you could offer an alliance partner.

 WHO?

List the marketing and visibility assets you want an alliance partner to bring to the table.

What marketing and visibility assets would you like an alliance partner to bring to you and your company? Consider the list on page 84 and rate the importance of each **Yes** as **High**, **Medium**, or **Low**.

Bear in mind that the marketing and visibility assets you'd like an alliance partner to bring to the table may vary based on the type of alliance you decide to pursue and on the specific alliance partner.

Reminder

Photocopy the following form and insert it into your *Alliance Journal* before beginning. Keeping a clean original will permit you to use the SmartMatch Alliance worksheets many times!

MARKETING/VISIBILITY ASSETS CHECKLIST: MYSELF/MY COMPANY©

Marketing/Visibility Asset	Got it!
An E-newsletter with a large subscriber list	☐
A publication, magazine, or newsletter with a large circulation distributed in hard copy through the postal service	☐
The ability to write articles for E-newsletters or other publications	☐
Regular TeleForums delivered to individuals and businesses in my current and target PINS	☐
A comprehensive and powerful website that reflects best practices in my industry or profession	☐
A website with high visitor volume	☐
High sales volume through my online store	☐

Marketing/Visibility Asset	Got it!
Frequent trade show attendance with high visibility and exposure	☐
High visibility and a strong reputation within my PINS	☐
A radio or TV show	☐
Strong branding and name recognition	☐
A solid retail presence	☐
A powerful marketing and advertising engine that consistently strengthens my company's brand name	☐
A unique service or expertise that an alliance partner's clients would value	☐
A strong sales force with high sales volume potential	☐
A visionary leadership team committed to, and seriously interested in, alliances	☐
A consistent track record of success and profitability	☐

Q: As a small business, shouldn't I pursue alliances with companies that are roughly the same size as mine?

A: A: The magic of SmartMatch Alliances is the concept of the Exchange of Value or EOV. Because the alliance is based on an exchange of equal value, the size of the partners is irrelevant. With a properly structured EOV, each partner benefits from exposure to high-potential growth opportunities. This makes it possible—and easy!—to attract a SmartMatch Alliance partner who will highly value the alliance, regardless of the size of your company . . . or theirs.

Reminder

Photocopy the following form and insert it into your *Alliance Journal* before beginning. Keeping a clean original will permit you to use the SmartMatch Alliance worksheets many times!

MARKETING/VISIBILITY ASSETS CHECKLIST:
MY POTENTIAL ALLIANCE PARTNERS©

Marketing/Visibility Asset

	Wanted?		
	Yes!	Importance	No
An E-newsletter with a large subscriber list	☐	H M L	☐
A publication, magazine, or newsletter with a large circulation distributed in hard copy through the postal service	☐	H M L	☐

Marketing/Visibility Asset	Yes!	Wanted? Importance	No
The ability to write articles for my E-newsletter or other publications	☐	H M L	☐
Regular TeleForums delivered to individuals and businesses in my current and target PINS	☐	H M L	☐
A comprehensive and powerful website that reflects best practices in their industry or profession	☐	H M L	☐
A website with high visitor volume	☐	H M L	☐
High sales volume through an online store	☐	H M L	☐
Frequent trade show attendance with high visibility and exposure	☐	H M L	☐
High visibility and a strong reputation within my current and/or target PINS	☐	H M L	☐
A radio or TV show	☐	H M L	☐
Strong branding and name recognition	☐	H M L	☐
A solid retail presence	☐	H M L	☐
A powerful marketing and advertising engine that consistently strengthens the company's brand name	☐	H M L	☐
A unique service or expertise that my customers or clients would value	☐	H M L	☐
A strong sales force with high sales volume potential	☐	H M L	☐
A visionary leadership team committed to, and seriously interested in, alliances	☐	H M L	☐
A consistent track record of success and profitability	☐	H M L	☐

List your "Non-negotiables."

Your "Non-negotiables" are the qualities or factors you feel a potential alliance partner must have in order to form an alliance with you and your company.

Some examples:

- a strong reputation for integrity in business dealings and employee relations
- at least three to five years in business or in their particular profession
- a content-rich, user-friendly website
- products or services that are non-offensive
- clients, customers, and prospects that are a perfect fit for you and your organization
- products and services that mesh well with yours
- policies, practices, and a culture that match yours
- quality standards that mirror yours and your company's

Use these examples to guide your thinking as you complete the following chart.

Reminder

Photocopy the following form and insert it into your *Alliance Journal* before beginning. Keeping a clean original will permit you to use the SmartMatch Alliance worksheets many times!

MY NON-NEGOTIABLES©

_____

_____

_____

_____

_____

_____

_____

_____

_____

_____

Look inside your current and target PINS for high-potential alliance partners.

You began to consider your current and target PINS on page 31. Now you have enough background and information on SmartMatch Alliances to laser in on the highest potential alliance partners within your PINS.

Alliance partners find each other in a seemingly infinite number of ways . . . they are colleagues within their current and target PINS, vendors serving the same client base with non-competing products and services, or even supplier and customer, just to name a few.

Following are some ideas to guide your thinking about finding high-potential alliance partners. Read these ideas with an open mind. Think creatively about yourself, your business, your future, your "I wish" list. Then, complete the *Prime Alliance Partners Worksheet*© on page 93.

Finding High-Potential Alliance Partners

Consider building a SmartMatch Alliance with individuals and businesses with whom you share:

- **Clients or customers.** Your potential alliance partners offer your clients or customers products and services that do not compete with yours. For example, American Airlines teamed up with VISA to offer the AAdvantage VISA card. As a result, VISA Card customers earn frequent flyer miles toward American flights based on how much they charge on their VISA cards.

  Your potential alliance partners might also offer your clients or customers products and services that naturally complement yours. For example, Coaching Success partnered with a website portal for trainers and training companies to offer TeleForums using expert presenters. As another client example, a software company created a SmartMatch Alliance with a specialized publication so together they sold more software to their business readers.

- **Your niche or specialties.** Your potential alliance partners might offer a product or service to businesses in your niche or specialty. For example, a training organization might create a SmartMatch Alliance with a national advertising association to deliver advertising sales training.

You might consider exploring an alliance with—

- a book publisher that serves the industries or professions of your high-potential prospects
- a non-competing company that sells to the same individuals and/or businesses you're targeting in your PINS
- a non-competing company in your PINS that has a large E-newsletter and 20,000 subscribers who would benefit from your products or services
- a non-competing company with a website that your prospects visit frequently
- an organization with 30,000 members that serves your prospects' PINS
- a publication with 250,000 readers that your prospects, customers, and clients regularly read
- a person who is a center-of-influence within the industry or profession you're targeting. For example, the executive director of a 25,000-member professional organization.

Client/Customer Alliances

Your own clients or customers may also be high-potential alliance partners—sometimes even the highest potential partners! Many of our coaching clients have developed client or customer alliances, and the approach has its advantages: familiarity is one of them. Your clients know your products, services, and expertise, and you know theirs. A relationship exists, and this means trust has already been established.

Bear in mind, an alliance with one of your clients or customers falls into a unique category with specific steps and strategies all its own. The reason: these types of alliances change the chemistry and working dynamics of the relationship. Because they are evolving out of existing relationships and especially because strong strategic alliances are often developed with your very best customers, you must take extra care in approaching and working through the development of a client alliance. (See Client/Customer Alliances Built to Last on page 91).

Value-added resellers (VARs) are another possibility. VARs act both as customers (they buy a product from a supplier) and as distributors, selling that product to others. If you decide to pursue an alliance with a VAR, remember that your primary obligation is to keep your commitment to your customer or client. Do not let the alliance undermine this relationship by causing you to cut corners or otherwise fail to deliver on your original commitments!

Branding Alliances

In a special type of alliance called a branding alliance, partners in complementary businesses expand the visibility of each other's brand names. This relationship is predicated on each partner bringing a recognizable and reputable brand to the alliance. In fact, partners often find each other because of the positive reputation of the other's brand and its appeal to the PINS each alliance partner is focusing on.

In branding alliances, partners exchange their powerful brand images, loyal audiences, broad exposure, and marketing muscle. Consider Starbuck's cafes placed in Barnes & Noble bookstores. Starbucks has a powerful brand name and a loyal customer base. So does Barnes & Noble. When these brands and customers are exchanged in an alliance relationship, the benefits for each are pure dynamite. Starbuck's gets the Barnes & Noble traffic (people shopping for books stop in for coffee); Barnes & Noble gets the Starbuck's traffic (people dropping in for a cup of coffee do a bit of book-browsing—and buying!).

This is precisely the sort of EOV we refer to when we say that alliances are a 1+1=5 proposition! (And the difference between Starbuck's, Barnes & Noble, and you and your

Client/Customer Alliances Built to Last

Here are some success strategies for building a SmartMatch Alliance with a client or customer:

* Keep the lines clear. Distinguish client work from alliance work. Draw clear lines between the product or service you're committed to delivering for your client and your SmartMatch Alliance's EOV.
* Put the existing established relationship first. Don't let a newly-formed alliance damage a long-standing client or customer relationship. Don't sacrifice a good client relationship for the potential success of a strategic alliance. Remember, actual business and actual revenue supercede potential business and potential revenue.
* Keep your end of the bargain—and then some. Be super-responsive and fix even the smallest hint of a problem—right away. Demonstrate your respect for your client's ongoing and expanded commitment to you and faith in your company. Determine your SmartMatch EOV and then deliver . . . in spades! More than a "nice guy/gal" policy, this is smart business. Think in terms of preserving the current relationship. Again, actual business supercedes potential business!
* Make your partner's internal alliance champion shine. Do all you can to include your internal alliance champion in conversations and meetings. Publicly credit this person with making the alliance happen and with delivering the benefits of the alliance to your customer or client organization. This will benefit your internal champion . . . and your alliance!
* Start small. Create and commit to an EOV that's easy for both sides to deliver (e.g., a simple exchange of sales and marketing materials for "mutual display," or a sharing of one pilot TeleForum, an EOV with a short term end). Starting small will keep the SmartMatch Alliance uncomplicated and short term, key assets in your efforts to solidify your alliance relationship with this new, important partner in a somewhat-more-delicate-than-usual situation.

Q: What are just-in-time (JIT) alliances and why are they valuable?

A: A JIT alliance makes contact with clients, customers and prospects at the immediate point of their interest and openness to buy. JIT alliances are valuable because they promote action—that is, buying—without delay and often without competition.

For example:

1. Imagine your résumé service featured at monster.com and displayed on someone's computer screen the moment that person posts a résumé. A JIT alliance with no immediate competition.
2. Picture coffee shop customers receiving a coupon for your nearby bookstore as soon as they order their latte. In exchange, you are giving out coffee shop coupons to your bookstore customers. A JIT alliance with no immediate competition.

company is simply one of scale. These mega-corporations are using the same strategies and tactics available to you.)

Your Prime Alliance Partner

Set aside some time now to identify your prime alliance partners. Be certain to tackle the questions on the *Prime Alliance Partners Worksheet*© when your energy is at its peak and you have time to fully concentrate on your responses. Select the time of day when you do your best work. Give yourself time to relax, reflect, and dream as you complete this important worksheet.

Reminder

Photocopy the following form and insert it into your *Alliance Journal* before beginning. Keeping a clean original will permit you to use the SmartMatch Alliance worksheets many times!

PRIME ALLIANCE PARTNERS WORKSHEET©

Part 1: Your Profession/Industry

Refer to the following example as you complete Part 1 . . .

Jack is a business consultant, and his niche is financial services companies. His specialty is long-term business planning. Jack has taken the time to develop a relationship with Patricia, the executive director of an international business consultants' association. In addition, Jack realizes there are non-competitive companies selling their products and services to the financial services industry, such as Alexandra's large printing company, that specializes in this industry. Jack also partners with trainers, speakers, and business coaches (non-competitive, related professions). This gives Jack a prime set of PINS from which to form SmartMatch Alliances.

1. Your industry or profession_____ [e.g., Jack is a business consultant]

2. Your niche(s)_____ [e.g., financial services companies]

3. Your specialty(ies)_____ [e.g., long-term business planning]

4. Key players (individuals and businesses) and centers of influence in your industry or profession _____ [e.g., Patricia, the executive director of the consultant's association]

continued

5. "Nearby" but non-competitive companies selling to the same audience _____ [e.g., if you are Jack, a business consultant, a companion company might be Alexandra's printing company]

6. Three to five industries or professions related to yours _____ [e.g., if you are Jack, a business consultant, related industries or professions might be trainers, speakers, and business coaches]

7. Your product(s)/service(s) is/are: _____

8. What individuals need them most? _____

9. What businesses need them most? _____

10. What groups/organizations/associations need them most? _____

Part 2: Your Marketing Niche

Refer to the following example as you complete Part 2 . . .

Thomas is the vice president of marketing for a manufacturer of office furniture. One of his company's niches is new commercial office buildings. Thomas has made the investment in connecting with Gabriel, the executive director of a regional association of commercial real estate professionals. In addition, Thomas realizes there are noncompetitive companies selling their products and services to new commercial office buildings, so he has developed a relationship with Dick, the head of a large construction company that is a significant developer of commercial office buildings. Thomas also partners with space planners, interior designers, and computer network companies (non-competitive, related professions). This gives Thomas a prime set of PINS from which to form SmartMatch Alliances. He has also identified and listed his top ten clients and prospects for additional alliance opportunities.

1. High-potential clients and prospects in your marketing niche _____ [Thomas puts new commercial office buildings on his list]

2. Key players (individuals and businesses) and centers of influence in your marketing niche_____[be specific, e.g. Gabriel, the

executive director of a regional association of commercial real estate professionals]

3. "Nearby" or companion niches_____ [e.g., Dick, the head of a large construction company]

4. Three to five related industries or professions _____ [for Thomas: space planners, interior designers, and computer network companies]

5. Names of high-potential companies in related industries and nearby niches _____

Part 3: Your Specialties

Refer to the following example as you complete Part 3 . . .

Kenny is a business coach whose specialty is assessment testing for sales professionals. Kenny had taken the time to develop a relationship with Paul, the executive director of a sales and marketing association. In addition, Kenny realizes non-competitive companies are selling other services to sales organizations, such as Howard's leads services. Kenny also partners with trainers, speakers, and business coaches (non-competitive, related professions). This gives Kenny a prime set of PINS from which to form SmartMatch Alliances.

1. High-potential clients and prospects in your area of specialty_____[Kenny puts companies using assessments for making hiring decisions on his list]

2. Key players (individuals and businesses) and centers of influence in an industry or profession that would showcase your specialty area_____[be specific, e.g., Paul, the executive director of a sales and marketing association]

3. Related specialties _____ [e.g., for Kenny, training organizations specializing in negotiation skills]

4. Three to five industries or professions in which you can highlight your specialty. _____[e.g., Howard's leads services.]

Look through your responses and select five high-potential partners. List them in priority order on the *Finish Line! My Prime Alliance Partners*© Worksheet. Select your highest priority potential alliance—your "prime potential partner"—and use this high-potential partner for the balance of the SmartMatch Alliance process in this book.

Reminder

Photocopy the following form and insert it into your *Alliance Journal* before beginning. Keeping a clean original will permit you to use the SmartMatch Alliance worksheets many times!

FINISH LINE! MY HIGH-POTENTIAL ALLIANCE PARTNERS©

Company	Contact Name	Contact Information
1.		
2.		
3.		
4.		
5.		

HOW?

Determine an EOV for your prime potential partner.

Your next step is to think through the nature of the alliance with your prime potential partner, specifically what the EOV will be for this Smart-Match Alliance.

We move on now to the development of a specific EOV for an alliance with your prime potential partner. Bear in mind that the essential purpose of SmartMatch Alliances is to exchange visibility and marketing tools for mutual benefit in a low- to no-risk arrangement. As a result, alliances are infinite in their variety.

Following is a good list of potential EOV strategies to get you started.

> ### An Important Note from the Coaches
>
> Once you've completed the process for your prime potential partner, the second potential partner on your list moves up to "prime" status. Return to this page and work through the balance of the process with this next prime partner in mind.
>
> This is the method you'll repeat each time you're interested in exploring an alliance with the remaining high-potential partners on your *Finish Line!* List.

E-mail-Based Exchanges

(Note that the following EOVs can be adapted for traditional printed newsletters and correspondence mailed through the postal service if this is more appropriate for your SmartMatch Alliance.)

- Alliance partners showcase one another's products or services in their E-newsletter by including a mention of the other partner's name and products or services.

- Partners feature one another's articles in their E-newsletters.

- Each partner showcases the alliance and publicizes a shared event, like a TeleForum or a workshop.

Example

Company A: A training company

Company B: A company that provides services to training companies and their clients

The EOV: Each provides content for the other's E-newsletter. A and B both showcase their expertise,

---

Value + Scale = Wow!

Alliances with trade or professional associations offer many potential partners to the benefits of scale. Bring solid value to the table . . . and watch the magic!

Who's Who: Elaine is president of a training and speaking company with expertise in the multi-housing industry. A national apartment association's membership is comprised of property management professionals.

The Goals: Elaine's goal was to gain more visibility with apartment property management professionals. She contacted the association's executive director and learned that he was looking for a training professional to deliver valuable learning and information to members.

The EOV: Elaine formed a revenue-sharing SmartMatch Alliance with the association. She delivers training and speaking programs for a fee (Value) and for exposure to the association's large membership (Scale). The association receives a portion of the revenue she generates (Value) and increases its member value and satisfaction (and renewals and referrals! . . . Scale) at the same time.

The Win-Win: After an initial revision of the revenue-sharing percentages so both parties felt it would be profitable, Elaine is receiving a nice fee for her programs and adding new apartment property management clients as well. In exchange, the association is earning fees from its member educational programs and continually increasing member satisfaction and referrals.

The Takeaway: These SmartMatch Alliances have a natural Wow Factor of Value + Scale, and they also take on a natural momentum. This means the ongoing revenue and visibility builds and continues indefinitely!

Q: My potential alliance partner wants me to make an up-front monetary investment to get the alliance started. Should I?

A: Unless this investment is small in scope and equal from each party in the alliance, the request does not fit with the SmartMatch Alliance concepts of balance, win-win, and equal Exchange of Value.

double the number of subscribers that see their content, and increase the breadth of information they deliver to their own subscribers.

TeleForum-Based Exchanges

- Alliance partners develop and deliver free Tele-Forums to attract a large combined audience.
- Partners develop and deliver paid TeleForums and share the revenues.

Example

Company A: An athletic equipment company with an E-newsletter on fitness topics

Company B: A company that conducts TeleForums regularly for a wide variety of audiences on a range of topics

The EOV: B provides articles on topics of interest to A's readers. These articles are tied to and showcased on B's TeleForums. A's readers get a service that no one else is providing, and B gets additional TeleForum participants and revenue from A's subscriber list.

Website-Based Exchanges

- Alliance partners feature each other's URL and/or banner ads on their websites.

- Partners provide links to each other's websites.

- Partners provide joint ability to register for alliance events focused on generating mutual benefit.

- Partners create a new, shared website that showcases the benefits, products, and/or services of the Smart-Match alliance. Then, the alliance partners share the cost of building, maintaining, and marketing the website.

Example

Company A: A food gift-basket company

Company B: A florist

The EOV: A and B develop a joint website that showcases their combined offerings. Both send their own sub-scribers to the website for products and services that match their needs.

Sales Team-Based Exchanges

(Note that when you're developing a SmartMatch Alliance with a sales team-based EOV, it's essential to be crystal clear on incentives and compensation and which alliance partner will be paying what.)

- Alliance partners cross-train each other's sales people to cross-sell each other's products and services.

- Partners leverage one another's product offerings and sales teams to complement their own portfolios and sales teams.

Example

Company A: Sells application software (employee tracking) to human resources departments

Company B: Sells a human resources application (assessments) that Company A does not make

The EOV: A has a substantial sales force. B does not. A's sales force adds B's assessments to its portfolio of products and is therefore able to offer its clients/prospects a more complete line of human resources applications. B benefits from the size and reach of A's sales force.

Publication-Based Exchanges

(Note: The following EOVs refer to magazines, newspapers, business journals, and other publications.)

- Alliance partners co-author articles that showcase their SmartMatch Alliance.
- Partners together design display ads for the SmartMatch Alliance's products or services.
- When partners are quoted for publication, they mention their SmartMatch Alliance.
- Partners use the publication to point to the SmartMatch Alliance website, E-newsletter, TeleForums, etc.

Example

Company A: A distance learning organization

Company B: An association whose members benefit from various forms of distance learning

The EOV: B includes A's articles in the newsletter distributed to its members. A gets added exposure to a wide group of high-potential prospects. B adds to its membership benefits.

Radio/TV-Based Exchanges

- Alliance partners co-create and co-host a radio talk show or TV program which showcases their Smart-Match Alliance.

- Partners arrange and choreograph guest appearances on existing radio/TV shows so that each alliance partner benefits.

- Partners share in the cost of radio and/or TV time for the SmartMatch Alliance and may sell advertising time or sponsorships to fund it.

Example

Company A: A charitable organization

Company B: A radio station

The EOV: A wants exposure for its charitable activities to encourage donations. A creates a public service show about a topic of interest. B airs the show, which improves the radio station's image with its advertisers who then begin to view the station as community-minded and responsible. This helps to solidify B's relationships with these key advertisers. In parallel, A benefits from an increase in donations.

In Person-Based Exchanges

- Alliance partners introduce their SmartMatch Alliance to their own key centers of influence.

- An alliance partner speaks at a trade show or conference showcasing their SmartMatch Alliance.

- If one alliance partner has high visibility and/or frequent attendance at industry/professional events, the other alliance partner may supply materials, samples, and promotional items to be included or offered at the event.

Example

Company A: A training company delivering presentations

Company B: Authors and content experts whose work is aligned with the topics A delivers

The EOV: B's material is quoted and used in A's presentations. A receives powerful, targeted content, while B's materials are made available for sale at the back of the meeting room.

Shared Packaging-Based Exchanges

- Partners jointly package new software and other products for increased exposure and distribution.

- One alliance partner's sales material is included in the product package of the other.

- Alliance partners develop favorable pricing for customers who purchase both alliance partners' products or services together.

> ## An Important Note from the Coaches
>
> Our list of EOV suggestions is not in any particular order, and we're not suggesting that one EOV is better or more suitable than another. We encourage you to create an EOV that matches your needs and the needs of your prime potential partner. You may choose to use one of our EOV suggestions, or simply use the list to jumpstart your mindmapping effort, below.

Example

Company A: Manufactures and sells shoes

Company B: Manufactures and sells socks

The EOV: A and B package their products together and double the exposure each receives to high quality prospects who are in need of the other's product.

Reminder

Photocopy the following form and insert it into your *Alliance Journal* before beginning. Keeping a clean original will permit you to use the SmartMatch Alliance worksheets many times!

PRIME POTENTIAL PARTNER PROFILE©

1. Where do the customers of your prime potential partner live, shop, eat, work?

2. Why do your prime potential partner's clients, customers, or prospects need your products or services right now?

3. Which of your EOV vehicles would be of greatest interest to this prime potential partner? How compelling is this EOV?

4. What else can you offer or add to make this EOV even more irresistible?

5. What does this prime potential partner read? Who publishes these publications?

6. What trade/professional organizations does your prime potential partner join?

7. What radio programs does your prime potential partner listen to?

8. What websites does your prime potential partner visit?

9. What E-mail discussion groups does your prime potential partner participate in or facilitate/sponsor?

10. What other habits does this prime potential partner have that are germane to the development of a SmartMatch Alliance?

Answer each question carefully, using as much detail as possible.

Use the power of mindmapping to sharpen and maximize your EOV.

Mindmapping is a brainstorming technique that we use to help our coaching clients (and ourselves!) find alliance partners, create excellent EOVs, build joint programs, create a pipeline of SmartMatch Alliance possibilities, attract new business, handle daily business decisions and challenges, and even solve problems that may arise within a given alliance.

Here's the basic mindmapping technique:

Begin by scheduling 30 minutes of uninterrupted time with no distractions such as ringing telephones, loud noises or knocks at your office door. Open your *Alliance Journal* to a clean page and draw a circle in the center of the page.

Place the label "SmartMatch Alliance EOVs" in the center of this circle. Next, draw a number of straight lines around the circle, like the spokes of a bicycle wheel. Lastly, on each spoke, list EOV ideas. Do not edit or judge the ideas you are

placing on each spoke while you are brainstorming because we want you to generate as many ideas as possible.

If you're stumped or your EOV ideas are not flowing, take a break to refresh your mind or share your progress with your business coach, manager, or a friend or trusted advisor. Sometimes another person's perspective is just enough to get your creative juices flowing.

"I am not a businessman: I am an artist."

—Warren Buffett
Billionaire investor,
business leader . . . and artist!

Next, develop your action words. With your initial mind map complete, turn to another clean page in your *Alliance Journal* and list the first "spoke" topic in the center of a new large circle and draw another set of straight lines around this circle. These lines are now the action words for thinking creatively while sharpening your EOV. When building these action words, do not make any quick assumptions. Instead, remain open to unusual ideas or solutions. Try to look at these EOVs from a new perspective by asking yourself, "How will these EOVs help my alliance-ability and attract stronger alliance partners? How can I create more EOVs?"

Some of the best mindmapping occurs when we look to other industries, other professions, or other successful individuals and see what kind of EOVs they have used. Many great ideas are just inches from where you are standing this very minute, but you need to look closely and have your antenna up to see and hear them. Spark SmartMatch Alliance ideas and nourish new perspectives by reading trade or business magazines unrelated to your current industry. This practice will expose you to new ideas in other industries that will encourage even more creativity around your EOVs or other SmartMatch Alliance ideas.

Now comes the fun part! Take each of your mindmaps and put them in outline form. Next to each action word, place an action step and specify the exact date for completing each task or step. Also, if you are going to delegate portions of this project, include the name of each person who will be responsible for a specific step and be certain they receive a copy of

Five Steps to Building Trust in a Virtual Alliance

In a virtual alliance, partners don't share facilities, geography, employees, or finances. Instead, they interact with each other exclusively through E-mail, fax, Web-based presentations, and phone. Therefore, in a virtual alliance, you can seek out the best alliance partners for your current purposes—wherever they are in the world and for whatever time period the alliance works.

These "virtual relationships" work well when alliance partners have mastered certain essential skills. Here are some suggestions:

1. Be crystal clear about roles and expectations.
2. Respect each other's time. Keep phone conference appointments. Respond to E-mails within 12 hours, if possible, and never wait more than 24 hours to respond.
3. Remember that in a virtual relationship, you don't receive non-verbal communication clues, which means you may need to make more of an effort to be certain you've heard and been heard . . . clearly!
4. Know how you come across. "Tone of voice" counts, both on the telephone and via E-mail. Give your voice a personality through volume, timbre, pace, which means let your virtual partner "see" your enthusiasm, interest, and commitment through your voice.
5. Make sure your business systems, tools, and technology are in fine working order to minimize distractions from your important alliance work.

your mind map so they can be clear on the purpose of your request. Lastly, take the action steps you are going to personally complete and place them directly in your appointment book. By scheduling time for each step on this project you are bringing this alliance project to life.

Using the mindmapping technique, try combining EOVs from the list on page 97. Look for ways to add exposure for yourself and your company and your prime potential partner. What EOVs have the power to add significant depth to your SmartMatch Alliance?

Once you've completed your first mindmapping exercise, pause and reflect joyfully on what you have accomplished. This process is specifically designed to support your thinking process and will get easier and easier with practice. Mindmapping is meant to be fun and can be done in large groups, at your next big meeting, or any time you need to visualize ideas quickly!

Determine whether your EOV is a 1 + 1 = 5 idea.

Does your EOV have serious potential for both alliance partners? SmartMatch Alliances are 1 + 1 = 5 propositions, that is to say, when alliance partners meet, structure a solid EOV, and fulfill their commitments to one another with integrity and professionalism, the resulting success is not even additive . . . it's exponential!

Complete the *EOV Checkpoint*© checklist:

Reminder

Photocopy the following form and insert it into your *Alliance Journal* before beginning. Keeping a clean original will permit you to use the SmartMatch Alliance worksheets many times!

EOV CHECKPOINT©

Is your EOV a 1 + 1 = 5 idea? **Yes!**

Is this an exchange of marketing and visibility assets aimed directly at increasing exposure and sales for both alliance partners? ☐

Is it aimed at producing mutual benefit, i.e., do both parties win? ☐

Will there be proportional benefits for each alliance partner? ☐

Is it low- to no-risk for both alliance partners? ☐

Is this EOV leveragable and scalable? Can your resources easily expand and contract? ☐

Is each alliance partner going to benefit from a big enough and significant enough vehicle for enhanced visibility? ☐

When you can answer *Yes!* to each of these questions, you're on your way to building a successful SmartMatch Alliance. If there are some for which you are not able to check *Yes!*, make changes and adjustments to your alliance's EOV as needed.

Put it all together.

Complete the following table. This is your starting point for the balance of the SmartMatch Alliance process!

Reminder

Photocopy the following form and insert it into your *Alliance Journal* before beginning. Keeping a clean original will permit you to use the SmartMatch Alliance worksheets many times!

MY SMARTMATCH ALLIANCE©

My SmartMatch Alliance Partner	My Marketing/ Visibility Tools	My Alliance Partner's Marketing/Visibility Tools	Our EOV

You're ready for the next step! Now that you're clear on your EOV, be creative with your approach, be flexible in your thinking, form a SmartMatch Alliance with a great partner, and enjoy the fruits of your efforts. It's now time to **Analyze and Evaluate!**

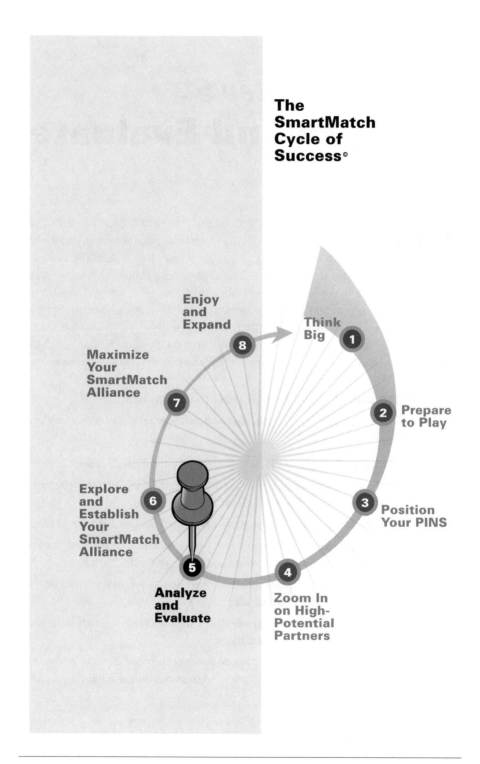

The
SmartMatch
Cycle of
Success©

Enjoy
and
Expand

Think
Big **1**

8

Maximize
Your
SmartMatch
Alliance

7

2 Prepare
to Play

Explore
and
Establish
Your
SmartMatch
Alliance

6

3 Position
Your PINS

5

4

Analyze
and
Evaluate

Zoom In
on High-
Potential
Partners

Step 5
Analyze and Evaluate

W e often advise coaching clients on the power of the Carpenter's Rule: "Measure twice, cut once" . . . also a suitable maxim to apply to the creation of SmartMatch Alliances. Though they are low- to no-risk, alliances still require diligent, thoughtful planning. You're investing time and energy in this powerful, strategic business-building effort, and you owe it to yourself, your company, and your potential partner(s) to maximize the value and impact of each alliance you create by thinking carefully and strategically.

Pause here and spend some time reflecting on the SmartMatch Alliance building process thus far and an alliance with your prime potential partner.

Learn more about your prime potential partner.

Gather as much information as you can about your prime potential alliance partner:

- Subscribe to their current E-newsletter and ask for back issues.
- Speak to those who might have established alliances with this partner in the past. How would they rate their experience?
- If the company is a public company, review its most recent annual report.
- Contact the company's industry and professional organizations, looking for anything you can learn about your prime potential partner.
- Visit this prime potential partner's website and assess its content, insights, ideas, and overall quality.
- After reviewing your prime potential partner's website, surf their links and note their partners and affiliates.
- Within a corporate structure, ask to meet with those directly above and below the person or team you are working with on the alliance.

Next, consider the potential quality of the relationship with this prime potential partner. Some general questions:

> *"Grain by grain, a loaf . . . stone by stone, a palace."*
> —George Bernard Shaw,
> *Author, dramatist, and literary critic*

- Are you professionally compatible? (Does communication flow easily? Do you see things in the same ways? Do you find humor in the same things?)

- Will negotiation and brainstorming be smooth, fast, and simple or more like pulling teeth?

- Have they built other alliances that succeeded?

Remember the *Alliance-Ability Checklist©* for determining your own level of alliance-ability? It's also a valuable tool for determining the alliance-ability of a potential alliance partner. The version of the *Checklist* below simply shifts the questions around to focus on your assessment of a potential partner's alliance-ability.

Reminder

Photocopy the following form and insert it into your *Alliance Journal* before beginning. Keeping a clean original will permit you to use the SmartMatch Alliance worksheets many times!

ALLIANCE-ABILITY CHECKLIST: MY PRIME POTENTIAL PARTNER©

Reputation and Skills   **Yes!**

Does your prime potential partner have a well-earned reputation for succeeding? ☐

Does your prime potential partner have a reputation for being trustworthy in business dealings? ☐

Does your prime potential partner have a sense of what a win-win relationship looks and feels like? ☐

Is your prime potential partner visible within his or her professions, industries, niches, and specialties (PINS)? ☐

Communication

Does your prime potential partner communicate effectively with others—verbally, in writing, through E-mail? ☐

Has your prime potential partner mastered the art of listening between the lines for important information and solid opportunities? Can he or she hear what is not said as well as what is said? ☐

Can your prime potential partner say, "Yesssss!"? (And can he or she say, "No thanks!"?) ☐

Does your prime potential partner reply to phone calls, faxes, and E-mails within 24 hours? ☐

Readiness Level   Yes!

Is your prime potential partner ready to take his or her business   ☐
and/or career to the next level?

Is your prime potential partner ready to think outside the box?   ☐

Does your prime potential partner want to make more money?   ☐

Is your prime potential partner flexible and open to new ideas?   ☐

Standards

Is your prime potential partner surrounded by a team   ☐
of superstars?

Do your prime potential partner's written materials have   ☐
a world-class image?

When something goes wrong, does your prime potential   ☐
partner fix it quickly?

Does your prime potential partner learn from your mistakes?   ☐

Does your prime potential partner keep his or her word?   ☐

Your Prime Potential Partner

Will an alliance with your prime potential partner be fun   ☐
and easy?

Does your prime potential partner believe in the power   ☐
of alliances?

Does your prime potential partner have the tenacity to pursue   ☐
an alliance he or she believes in?

Does your prime potential partner have the patience to see   ☐
the alliance commitment through to the end?

Now, count your Yeses . . .

18 to 21:

Your partner is absolutely alliance-able! What are you waiting for?!

12 to 17:

You may need to postpone creating this alliance.

0 to 11:

This is most likely not a high-potential alliance.

Discuss your SmartMatch Alliance with people whose views you respect and trust. Ask for candid feedback.

In the corporate world, this feedback would come from an organization's board of directors, executive committee, peer group, mentor, or team members. For small businesses, we recommend creating a personal board of directors. For more information on how to build a personal board of directors, go to our website at http://www.coachingsuccess.com/articles.

Make your choice or decision regarding your potential SmartMatch Alliance and write a brief summary statement to yourself in your *Alliance Journal* explaining the reasons for your decision. Refer to this page of your Journal if you need to be reminded of the reasons behind a critical decision pertaining to your SmartMatch Alliance.

Lastly, mark your calendar for some point in the future to revisit and re-evaluate your decisions and choices.

Now that you've mulled over your SmartMatch Alliance, done your due diligence, and gathered feedback from your trusted advisors, you're ready to **Explore and Establish Your First SmartMatch Alliance.**

The SmartMatch Cycle of Success©

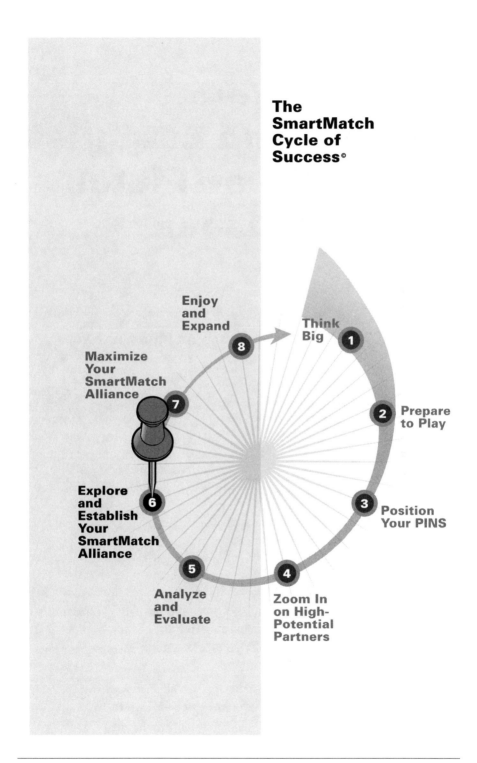

Enjoy and Expand

8

Think Big

1

Maximize Your SmartMatch Alliance

7

Prepare to Play

2

Explore and Establish Your SmartMatch Alliance

6

Position Your PINS

3

Analyze and Evaluate

5

Zoom In on High-Potential Partners

4

Step 6

Explore and Establish Your SmartMatch Alliance

Y ou're ready now to begin actively exploring an alliance with your prime potential partner.

Begin the alliance conversation with a call or in-person meeting.

Observe these guidelines for this initial communication:

An Important Note from the Coaches

At this point, we assume you've had some contact with your prime potential partner such as an in-person meeting at an industry event, a phone call, or an exchange of E-mails. Therefore, the following guidance applies to the start of your *detailed* Smart-Match Alliance conversations with your prime potential partner, rather than your initial contact.

- Let your enthusiasm shine through.

- Approach the communication as an exploration, be open to new ideas, and be flexible, willing to look at creative ideas.

- Begin by presenting the benefits . . . the mutual gains you identified in the process of designing this SmartMatch Alliance.

- Ask your potential partner to share ideas and feedback on how an alliance might work.

- Describe the proportional benefits for each alliance partner. For example, will the revenue be shared 10-90, 90-10, or 50-50? And why?

- Be specific about what each of you will bring to the alliance.

- Discuss possible time frames for an initial or pilot alliance project.

Have exploratory conversations. Explain why the ideal time to explore this alliance is . . . right now!

Here is a sample of alliance correspondence we initiated in the hopes of forming a SmartMatch Alliance between Coaching Success, our own alliance, and a major national business publication with a circulation of more than 1.5 million subscribers:

Dear [name of potential alliance partner],

Great speaking with you earlier today. We hope the information below provides some additional clarity on how our companies might work together.

It seems clear that [publication] readers are active and lifelong learners. It's also clear that your publication has achieved incredible success in a short period of time because of your high-impact, innovative, and aggressive approach.

By adding TeleForums (a telephone conference call with 10 to 100 participants) as an ancillary service, you could offer your subscribers a unique opportunity to have an interactive learning experience. This service would also tie your subscribers more closely to your publication while providing a new revenue stream for [publication] . . . consistent with your corporate goals.

I hope this message serves the purpose of forwarding our dialog. What might our next step be?

Best Regards,

Judy and Ernest
Coaching Success™

SmartNote

To end well, start smart. Invest the time and effort on the front end of your Smart-Match Alliance building process to establish clear roles, accountabilities, success factors, and timing.

Second Contact

If your prime potential partner continues to be interested, initiate a second contact in which you outline precisely how the SmartMatch Alliance would work.

Some guidelines for this communication:

- Restate the goals of the alliance and the mutual gains of the EOV.

A SmartMatch Made in Heaven?

When you and your alliance partner are ready to launch your first alliance, consider a pilot program to test your idea and the strength of the SmartMatch Alliance you've designed.

There are a variety of ways to accomplish this, including:

- A stand-alone pilot to test the market, get used to working together, introduce a new concept, etc. This would be a one-time project, as contrasted with "first in a series" or "more to come."
- A simple or modest plan for an ongoing series of ads, events, TeleForums, articles, etc. This approach is ideal for starting small, with the intention of ramping up your SmartMatch Alliance as you learn from the market and gauge what is successful.

And don't miss opportunities to devise your own "risk-free experiments" for introducing and growing your SmartMatch Alliances!

- Be crystal clear about roles within the alliance . . . who will do what and when.

- Specify your "must-haves" and non-negotiables (review your "Non-Negotiables" list in your Alliance Journal) . . . the qualities or factors a potential alliance partner must have in order for the alliance discussion to continue.

- Ask for agreement that each alliance partner will respond to the other via fax/E-mail/phone within 24 hours.

- Re-confirm your EOV and discuss the specifics of the value exchange that will move the alliance forward.

Here is the second contact we had with the same business publication about a potential SmartMatch Alliance between our companies:

Dear [name of potential alliance partner:]

Many thanks for your quick response!

We're delighted to know you're interested in learning more about our ideas for structuring and conducting a SmartMatch Alliance between our companies.

Here are some ideas about how an alliance between our organizations might work:

- Our Coaching Success TeleForums™ would be marketed to your current magazine subscribers and website visitors.
- Our Coaching Success TeleForums™ would be marketed to new [publication] subscribers and to others in your database.
- In addition, we will promote these TeleForums on our website and to our extensive E-newsletter lists, with subscribers in 70-plus countries.

- We can discuss the exciting possibilities for promoting special high-profile presenters, including your key advertisers as well as writers and authors.
- To guarantee the quality of each TeleForum, we will coach all presenters in our proven methods and successful formats honoring the best in adult distance learning.
- Once a [publication] participant has enrolled for a Tele-Forum, Coaching Success™ will handle the confirmation and call instructions, the database entry, the payment by credit card, the roster for each call and a post-call follow-up . . . inviting them to future TeleForums.
- We will share revenues from alliance activities 50-50 and reconcile monthly.

We feel each of our companies has a great deal to gain by proceeding, and we look forward to our next conversation.

May we hear from you again this week?

Best Regards,

Judy and Ernest
Coaching Success™

Special Note on International Alliances

For complex or international alliances, be certain each alliance partner has a clear understanding of the complex cultural differences among companies, individuals, markets, and countries, and how they can be resolved.

Next Step

The next step is your prime potential partner's. He or she must review your idea for the alliance, request any changes, and respond to you and your company.

Continue to exchange letters, calls, and/or E-mails until you're both sufficiently comfortable that the SmartMatch Alliance itself and the EOVs are appropriate and have a high potential for each partner.

At this stage, you must be working to establish firm guidelines for:

- deliverables (e.g., marketing materials, website copy, E-newsletter samples, actual products, and/or a sample of the service provided)

- alliance activity start and end dates (building in enough time so that all contingencies can be covered with ease and grace . . . and so that you're easily able to keep your commitments)

- process checkpoints (the points between start and end dates at which alliance partners will have a detailed communication on the progress of the SmartMatch Alliance)

- some understanding about the expected duration of the alliance

- ground rules for working together (the ways in which alliance partners will communicate, including specific communication channels such as conference calls, E-mails, letters, faxes, etc.)

- each partner's accessibility and responsiveness (hours of operation, calls/E-mails returned in 24 hours or less, etc.)

- a shared level of high standards around timing for responses, service level to clients and customers, quality of written materials, etc.

- how and when flexibility may be needed with this SmartMatch Alliance (Even though at this point alliance partners are being specific about roles and responsibilities, still be open to new risk-free experiments and encourage your alliance partner to have a flexible point of view too.)

- the revenue-generating versus non revenue-generating portions of the alliance (This might mean that part of the alliance with your SmartMatch Alliance partner will include bringing many more visitors to their website, which is the non revenue-generating portion of the alliance. The revenue-generating portion of the alliance begins when these website visitors are at the website purchasing products or services or registering for a paid TeleForum.)

- the reach and repetition with each alliance initiative (Reach refers to the number of possible buyers, clients, customers, or prospects who know about your product or service. Repetition refers to the frequency with which people in your potential market hear from you and learn about your alliance offerings.)

- who will make website adjustments and revisions (Generally, each party takes care of his or her own website revisions, with collaboration where needed for consistency. If there is a joint website for the SmartMatch Alliance, there is usually one designated webmaster.)

In the end, you should have a brief written SmartMatch Alliance agreement that states clearly what each alliance partner will do for the other. Ideally, the agreement is a useful reference tool before, during, and after the alliance and leaves no room for interpretation about what each alliance partner will provide.

Here's a sample:

Alliance Partners:

Exchange of Value [EOV]:

Start Date:

End Date:

Special Considerations: _____

_____

On ____date _____, we agree to evaluate our results
make any necessary or desired changes before proceeding further.

Signed _____ and _____

Date _____

Should an attorney review the agreement?

This is a common question: should alliance partners spend
the time and money to have an attorney create a formal legal
contract before getting started? You certainly can make this
investment if you like, and we do advise you and your company to build some form of written agreement, whether
formal or informal. But keep in mind that when a Smart-
Match Alliance is properly structured, it's low- to no-risk,
limiting either partner's legal exposure. Often, a simple E-
mail and a handshake . . . even a virtual one . . . seem to do the
trick quite nicely.

As you become more experienced with alliances and
develop more complex ones and even expand into international
waters, attorney involvement might be a good investment of
time and resources. Again, remember the beauty of a powerful
SmartMatch Alliance is speed and simplicity. Keep things as
simple as possible—it's more fun this way!

Congratulations! Time to stop and celebrate! Your first
SmartMatch Alliance is in place . . . but don't stop here! Go
build two more!

And keep your alliance vibrant and evolving by following the guidelines in the next section to **Maximize Your
SmartMatch Alliance.**

SmartNote

Carefully craft and
manage your communi-
cations with your
alliance partners, espe-
cially anything that has
to do with roles and
responsibilities and
your EOV. Commit as
much as possible to
writing. E-mails are
especially advanta-
geous because they
instantly and asynchro-
nously create a perma-
nent record of a corre-
spondence stream.

SmartMatch Alliance
partners must have,
above all else, flaw-
less communication.
Be clear. Leave
nothing open to inter-
pretation. When it
doubt, communicate!

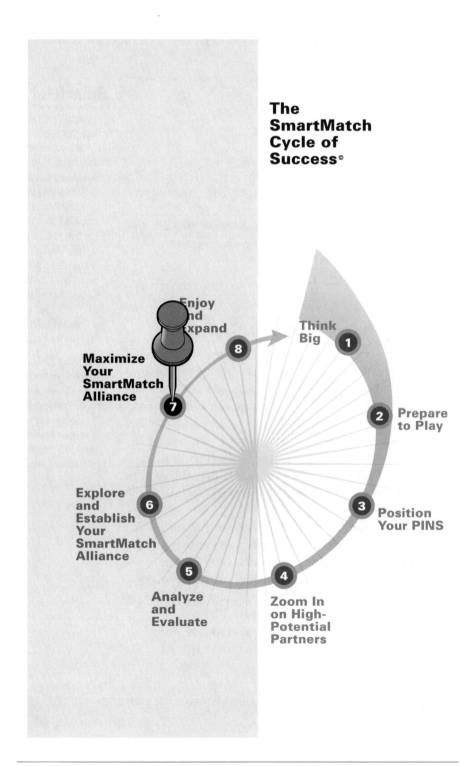

The
SmartMatch
Cycle of
Success©

Enjoy
and
Expand

Think
Big **1**

8

Maximize
Your
SmartMatch
Alliance

7

Prepare
to Play **2**

Explore
and
Establish
Your
SmartMatch
Alliance **6**

3 Position
Your PINS

5

4

Analyze
and
Evaluate

Zoom In
on High-
Potential
Partners

Step 7
Maximize Your SmartMatch Alliance

I t's time to move forward with your SmartMatch Alliance with your new partner.

First, be a good alliance partner.

Some crucial guidelines:

- Uphold your end of the EOV.

- Adhere to all deadlines for deliverables as well as process checkpoints. For example, don't promise brochure copy for Friday, and then fail to deliver until Tuesday.

- Redirect as needed based on what you discover during the process checkpoints. For example, don't run off on vacation with your promised E-newsletter unwritten, and be unreachable by phone.

Use your *Alliance Journal* to "keep score" on the ongoing health and success of your SmartMatch Alliance. Answer these questions as objectively as possible on a fresh, clean page in your Journal:

- Compare actual with desired outcomes: What EOV were you to receive from this specific alliance? (Refer to My SmartMatch Alliance©, page 110.) Are you realizing the value and desired outcomes from this alliance?

- Was this value delivered to you by your alliance partner? What were your desired outcomes for alliances in general? (Look back in your *Alliance Journal* for your answers to the "Why?" question we posed on page 79.) Are you realizing the value and desired outcomes from this SmartMatch Alliance?

SmartNote

Keep your sense of humor. Humor is a great antidote to tensions, and when alliance partners can laugh together, it makes it easier to ride the peaks and valleys of the alliance relationship.

- Measure the success of the alliance: how many leads, new customers or clients are you getting? Has there been an increase in your revenues?

- Are you enjoying your work with this alliance partner?

Watch for signs an alliance isn't working or might be in jeopardy:

- Your alliance partner doesn't produce agreed-upon deliverables or does so half-heartedly.

- Your partner doesn't return phone calls or E-mails promptly.

- The business climate for your alliance partner is rapidly changing, and this might affect your partner's ability to uphold the EOV you both agreed to.

- The working dynamic or chemistry isn't positive, uplifting, and growth-inspiring.

- You're spending a disproportionate amount of time on the alliance . . . more than you think you should or thought you'd have to spend.

- Add to this list any events, circumstances, or general feelings that the alliance is too hard or not promising. When in doubt, go with your gut!

Take action

If the alliance isn't working, act swiftly. Spend some time considering which pieces are not working and why. Work proactively with your alliance partner to solve problems if possible. Re-communicate processes and standards.

If you still cannot resolve the issues that are vexing you, give your alliance partner 30-days notice that you intend to exit the alliance. Keep your exit light and easy ("This is just not a workable match for me right now"). Thank your partner, wish them the best . . . and continue to look for more SmartMatch Alliances!

Behind the Scenes

A national computer rental company specializing in large events creates an alliance with a hardware supplier to build a local presence around the world.

Who's Who: A Coaching Success client provides rental computers and software and technical support services for trade shows, conferences and major events. A computer hardware supplier has branches around the world.

The Goals: The rental company wanted to grow by providing clients who have multiple show dates, tight budgets, special time requirements, high volume needs, or unique constraints with a national rental program for equipment that meets high quality standards. The hardware company was looking to increase revenue.

The EOV: The hardware supplier acts as the rental company's local presence in exchange for a percentage of equipment rental revenue.

The Win-Win: To make this SmartMatch Alliance work, both companies invested lots of time and attention to alliance processes and standards. The hardware supplier appears to be a branch office of our client's computer rental company. As a result, the relationship between the two companies is transparent to their customers and both companies have increased their revenues. Plus, the alliance required no additional capital investment in computer rental inventory for our clients.

The Takeaway: Be clear on all roles up front, including standards, revenue sharing, and processes.

SmartNote

If you sense your alliance partner isn't delivering for any reason, act! Trust your intuition, hunches, inklings and reactions. If something sounds too good to be true, or just doesn't feel right, exit—gracefully—but do exit.

Example: A company that promises to broad-cast your message to 300,000 of their E-newsletter subscribers (all "qualified prospects")—next week. But in reality only 1,500 people were going to receive the initial announcement.

When all goes well, some of your SmartMatch Alliance will come to a natural and graceful end. Celebrate success with your alliance partner and end on a note of mutual respect and gratitude for what you both gained.

Other alliances will continue for years and years—so enjoy!

And always learn from the experience. Take out your Alliance Journal and write down three key learnings you gleaned from this SmartMatch Alliance. Refer to these learning points as you **Enjoy and Expand** with additional alliances in the future.

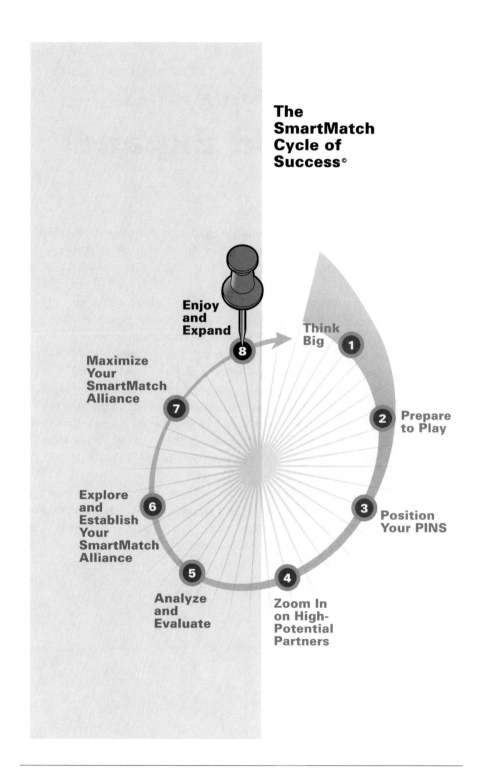

The
SmartMatch
Cycle of
Success©

Enjoy
and
Expand

8

Think
Big 1

Maximize
Your
SmartMatch
Alliance

7

Prepare
to Play 2

Explore
and
Establish
Your
SmartMatch
Alliance

6

Position
Your PINS 3

5

4

Analyze
and
Evaluate

Zoom In
on High-
Potential
Partners

Step 8
Enjoy and Expand!

At this point we hope you're enjoying the success from your first Smart-Match Alliance. Continue to use your *Alliance Journal*, looking for patterns of success, areas of opportunity, and any pitfalls that many have arisen along the way.

Notice which specific methods and techniques worked best for your Smart-Match Alliance, since each alliance is unique. These are the points you will reinforce, repeat, and enhance for future SmartMatch Alliances.

It is time to look for other alliance possibilities. Remember that now you know the ropes! Your SmartMatch Alliance will form faster and more easily because you understand the steps, stages, and pitfalls. You'll find your revenues growing faster because you've increased your understanding of the principles of the EOV. In addition, you have more confidence about your ability to structure a winning strategic alliance, and this confidence will shine through. Trust with each new alliance partner will build faster because you'll be able to reference existing successful alliances.

Continually raise your standards in your search for future prime potential partners. Reach deeper into your current and target PINS. Become more involved in professional organizations and align yourself more strategically with high-potential alliance partners. Remember, the deeper and the longer you are within your PINS, the more frequently new alliance partners will be contacting *you*.

Hand in Hand

How two consulting firms joined forces to serve the same clients and increase revenues.

Who's Who: Our Coaching Success client, a successful information technology (IT) consulting firm, was seeking growth. A software sales company provides systems software for enterprise-wide distribution of applications.

The Goals: The IT firm wanted to increase their market share and gain greater exposure among technology executives within their target companies. The software company was also seeking growth.

The EOV: The consulting firm sells its services using the software company's sales force. In exchange, the software company's sales force receives an attractive commission-based compensation program.

The Win-Win: The consulting firm's revenues are increasing and the software company's sales force is happy with the extra product in their portfolio and the additional commission it generates.

The Takeaway: This is a good example of a "horizontal" SmartMatch Alliance that enables alliance partners to increase their visibility and exposure in their target markets and to provide additional services to their prospects and clients.

three

Taking on Tomorrow

> *"Nothing unless first a dream."*
>
> —CARL SANDBURG, AMERICAN 20TH CENTURY POET

*A*t the beginning of SMARTMATCH ALLIANCES, we promised you a strategy for getting better prospects to come to you, in greater numbers, faster than ever before.

We've taken you step-by-step through this process and hope by now you're well on your way to building alliances that will enable you to take on tomorrow with power and confidence . . . and create the business and life of your dreams.

We'd like to leave you with one final word: persist! Remember the time-honored maxim: "If at first you don't succeed, you're like most people!" Keep at it! Your first SmartMatch Alliance may not be your best, but your third, fourth, and fifth will bring you business expansion possibilities beyond measure.

And each one—from your first to your 101st—will teach you something and bring you another step closer to new heights of success.

Finally, thank you for traveling this road together with us. We hope you've enjoyed the journey as much as you'll enjoy the business-expanding success of SmartMatch Alliances.

We'd love to hear from you . . . so come visit us at www.coachingsuccess.com and drop us a note about your SmartMatch Alliance building experiences.

Until then, we wish you the very best.

Ordering Information

For easy, secure online ordering go to **www.coachingsuccess.com/books** OR
You may fax the following form to our secure fax line at 435-615-8670.

Orders will be shipped within 48 hours.

Please send me _____ copies of *SmartMatch Alliances*™ at $19.95 USD per copy plus $4.95 for shipping and handling.

Total Amount To Be Charged _____

Credit Card [PLEASE CIRCLE YOUR CHOICE]   MasterCard   VISA   American Express

Credit Card Number   _____

Expiration Date   _____

Cardholder Signature   _____

Cardholder Name [PLEASE PRINT]   _____

Shipping Information

Name: _____

Company: _____

Address: _____

City, State, Zip   _____

E-mail Address   _____

Telephone Number   _____

Volume Discounts

To inquire about volume discounts [for 50 or more copies] for your company or organization send an E-mail to books@coachingsuccess.com.

SmartMatch Alliance Journal™

To order a companion SmartMatch Alliance Journal(tm) for immediate download as a PDF file go to www.coachingsuccess.com/books.

SmartMatch Alliance Brokering

We assist companies and organizations in creating powerful SmartMatch Alliances.

For more information about alliance brokering send an E-mail to alliancehelp@coachingsuccess.com and tell us about what kind of alliance you would like to develop.